as

le

May 2015

KEYS *to*

VICTORY

MICHAEL A. BROWN

CONTENTS

i

FOREWORD

When I was a young minister in my twenties, I invited a man then in his eighties to speak at my church. His name was Joseph Smith and he was one of the earliest leaders of our Movement. Although it was over forty years ago, I still remember the question he asked my congregation, "How many of you sitting here want to experience spiritual victory in your life?"

Unsurprisingly every hand went up.

Looking everyone in the eye he said, "Be careful what you wish for, for victory presupposes a battle."

There are three major spiritual battles mentioned in Scripture. The first is Christ's battle against the Devil that was won at the cross. The last is the battle of Armageddon mentioned in the book of Revelation – a war that really does end all wars. The third battle is the war of the flesh against the spirit that in its various forms is addressed by the apostle Paul in his epistles.

It is this vital subject that this book by Mike Brown addresses. Understanding the rules of engagement, the strategy of our enemy and the power at our disposal makes the difference between us living as victims or living in victory.

Positional triumph has to be married to experiential victory if we are to live at the level that God intended for us and fully claim our destiny.

When America passed the law that all slaves were emancipated, on paper no one needed to remain in bondage. However, for that freedom to be felt, those had been liberated had to hear the truth that they were free and make a decision, however much they were intimidated, to live fully and expansively as free men and women.

In the pages that follow you will read about the positive consequences of the cross – a finished work that makes us 'more than conquerors.' You will also learn that appropriating victory in our own lives depends on fighting from the position of strength that Christ has secured for us, putting on the whole armour of God and embracing what can only be called a 'security system for the soul' that keeps us alert to the Devil's schemes. God has only got good plans for us, but the Enemy has other ideas.

John Glass

General Superintendent
Elim Foursquare Gospel Alliance

Spring 2015

INTRODUCTION

MANY books have been written on the subject of foundations for the Christian life. Although it is true that some of the chapters in this book deal with foundational issues in the Christian life and walk (such as repentance and being filled with the Holy Spirit, for example), yet the book is not intended to be specifically about foundations. Over the course of my ministry as a pastor and teacher, I have come to understand that there are specific areas in which it can be difficult to practise the word of God and to overcome issues, or which may be problematic for us, and which can affect our walk with the Lord, if we do not learn how to approach or deal with them properly. It is such areas (including some foundational ones) that this book attempts to address.

Over the years, I have seen simply too many believers get caught in the trap of bitterness and unforgiveness, for example, or who struggle to really trust God in their circumstances, or who live such consistently busy lives that they have problems learning to practise basic spiritual disciplines, with the result that their spiritual lives never really seem to take off and grow as they should, and so on. Any experienced pastor would probably agree that these are areas that they deal with time after time in believers' lives when counselling them.

So this book attempts to address areas such as these (including some foundational topics). Apart from chapter 2 (on the meaning of the cross), the aim is not to lay theological or doctrinal foundations

1

for the Christian life (although there is certainly plenty of theological truth in the various chapters), so much as to address experiential and relational issues which can lay the groundwork for healthy spiritual and relational growth in the community of God's people, providing us with keys to victory.

Chapter 1, on 'doing life' with Jesus, is introductory to the rest of the book, and from then on each chapter deals with a different topic (although some are clearly related to others). The different chapters, therefore, can be read individually and the book approached piecemeal, as it were. Over the years, the topics addressed have been taught many times in church meetings and Bible study groups, and also, as I said above, in counselling situations with individual believers. The book, therefore, is the fruit of much time and labour and is aimed to be a complement to ongoing, regular teaching ministry. It can be used by individual believers reading on their own at home, or used for group discussions in relaxed fellowship environments (although it is not specifically designed for group study), and can be useful to young believers, to those further on in their walk in the Way, and also to church leaders.

The texts of different chapters have been read by believers in our own church, and the feedback from them in every case has always been encouraging. I am well aware that each of the chapters could be expanded to become a book in its own right, so I have simply tried to address the gist of the issue in each case. At some points, I have inserted specific readings from the Bible, and the reader would do well to read these, as doing so will enhance his/her understanding of what is being discussed in the related chapter. Similarly, many Bible verses have been written into the text to help with understanding.

However, many other verses are simply referenced, but it would still help the reader to look these up and read them at the relevant points.

Over the course of a lifetime, some of the issues addressed are faced by us all as believers from time to time, and it is good to have a resource to hand that can remind us of basic principles that need to be working in our lives in such times. Although we can indeed learn lessons about walking with God through life in any particular one-off experience, such lessons are learnt properly and mastered over the course of going through similar experiences several times.

So, as my dear wife commented one day, this is 'a book for life' which can be picked up as need arises and individual chapters read over again, to encourage and strengthen us as we learn and grow in the 'warp and woof' of life experience. I am also aware that other chapters could be written which also give us keys to victory (and perhaps these could become part of another book), but, certainly, getting hold of these present chapters and seeing the principles and teachings expounded therein working in our life, will cause us to see victory in several different areas of our walk.

I hope that you as a reader are blessed and strengthened by this book, and I commend it to you in the confidence that *'he who began a good work in you will carry it on to completion until the day of Jesus Christ'* (Phil. 1:6).

Pastor Michael A. Brown

Spring 2015

1

DOING LIFE WITH JESUS

'"Come, follow me," Jesus said' (Matt. 4:19)

'If you hold to my teaching, you are really my disciples. Then you will know the truth, and the truth will set you free' (John 8:31-32)

HEARING the words "Come, follow me," from the mouth of Jesus began an encounter for the early disciples which proved to be life-changing for them. As they followed this simple invitation, it led them into a relationship with him which eventually transformed them.

Jesus did not invite them into living a life which would be simply religious; nor was it an invitation into living a life in which they professed faith, but then walked in daily life in a way which was little different to that of unbelievers; nor was it about creating a merely intellectual understanding of a walk of faith. It was an invitation to live in relationship with him daily; to hear and absorb his radical teaching about the kingdom of God; to discuss this teaching with him and to learn how to put it into practice in their lives; to observe the power and glory of his miracles, and to be mentored and trained into doing the same kind of ministry which he himself was doing.

5

As Jesus presented himself and proved himself to them as the living Son of God, what they saw and heard was deeply experiential and life-applied. The whole purpose of his ministry and teaching was to lead them into a life of living faith as they lived in daily relationship with him, and to be transformed as they learned to submit themselves to living life in the kingdom of God, applying its radical teaching and values to every aspect of their lives, as he taught them. **It was an invitation to learn how to 'do their lives' with Jesus.**

Building on the bedrock

Reading: Matthew 7:24-27

In Matthew 7:24-27, Jesus used the well-known illustration of two men building houses for themselves: one built on rock and the other built on sand. When the storms of life came, both of these houses were tested. The first remained standing, because it was built on the solid ground of the rock which the storms could not destroy, while the second was destroyed simply and precisely because its foundation was built on sand which was washed away during the storms. **Jesus likened the man who built on the rock to a man who builds his life by putting his (i.e. Jesus') words into practice** (Matt. 7:24).

It stands to reason in life experience that a house which has a weak foundation or a foundation which goes awry, is a house which will have difficulty in remaining standing or which will need major repair work on its foundation at some stage – and, although not impossible, this is always a very difficult job to do, requiring much time and expense. Similarly, the foundation itself (and as a consequence the house) will not be secure if it is built on soft ground. So the foundation needs to be built on solid, hard ground which will not give way underneath the foundation; this is the bedrock.

The New Testament employs several 'building' metaphors concerning Jesus (along with the many other metaphors that are used of him in Scripture). He is the **only foundation** of our faith (1 Cor. 3:11); his teachings are **the bedrock** upon which the house of our faith is built (Matt. 7:24-27); he is the **chief cornerstone** (Eph. 2:20, 1 Peter 2:6) and **the capstone** (1 Peter 2:7), and so on. As an old hymn says: 'He is the rock on which I build, my shield and hiding place.' Hence, in order to attempt to build a Christian life which will be able to resist the challenges of the storms and floods of life, we not only need to build a strong foundation, we also need to make sure that we build that foundation on solid bedrock, the person, work and teachings of Jesus Christ.

There are some particular teachings which are described in the New Testament as being **foundational** to our spiritual lives. These are also called **elementary teachings** and are listed in Hebrews 6:1-2 as **repentance from dead works** (or, useless religious rituals), **faith in God, instruction about baptisms, the laying on of hands, the resurrection of the dead**, and **eternal judgement**. This particular group of early Hebrew believers were exhorted to master these foundational aspects of the faith and to move on from them and grow into Christian maturity (Heb. 6:1). However, in their case, the writer rebukes them for their spiritual lethargy and consequent slow growth in mastering these foundational teachings (Heb. 5:11-14).

The motif of 'building' is also used in several parts of the New Testament to describe the growth of our Christian lives. For example, God is described as being **the builder of everything** (Heb. 3:4). As believers we are together called **God's building** (1 Cor. 3:9) and we are **being built together as living stones** (1 Peter 2:5) into becoming **a temple** (2 Cor. 6:16) in which God dwells, built upon **the foundation** of the apostles and prophets (Eph. 2:19-22). Paul likened his work as an apostle and teacher to that of **a master builder** or **an expert builder** (1 Cor. 3:10). He laid the foundations of faith in the lives of believers, while other teachers would also later build upon that foundation (1 Cor. 3:10).

Putting the word of God into practice

'Therefore everyone who hears these words of mine and puts them into practice is like a wise man who built his house upon the rock'
(Matt. 7:24)

So the New Testament exhorts us to lay good, solid foundations for this building of our spiritual lives, and to build these on the bedrock of Christ's teachings. However, it is not simply hearing (or reading) and therefore cognitively knowing Jesus' words which builds up our lives as believers, **it is the putting of them into practice which actually builds and transforms us**. When Luke stated that the early believers *'devoted themselves to the apostles' teaching'* (Acts 2:42), he did not mean that the believers merely listened regularly to what the apostles taught. The word 'devoted' means 'to be earnest towards', 'to persevere in,' 'to be constantly diligent with,' or 'to adhere closely to,' and so it also suggests their learning to put this teaching into practice as it interfaced with their daily lives (cf. Acts 2:44-45). Similarly, the apostolic teaching throughout the epistles **is applied to daily life and daily relationships**.

This emphasis on putting the word of God into practice in situations of daily life, and therefore actually 'doing daily life' with Jesus, can be found in several passages in the New Testament. As stated above, Jesus said that such a person is building the house of his life on solid ground (Matt. 7:24). He also said that real, life-applied discipleship as a follower of Jesus lies in 'holding to' or 'remaining in' (i.e. believing and practising as a lifestyle) his teaching: *'If you hold to my teaching, you are really my disciples'* (John 8:31).

Similarly, the apostle Paul said that it is by speaking the truth in love that we build ourselves up, grow and mature together (Eph. 4:15-16). James also emphasizes our need to continue to look intently into the word of God, and to put into practice what we have understood from it, rather than simply forgetting it:

'Do not merely listen to the word, and so deceive yourselves. Do what it says. Anyone who listens to the word but does not do what it says is like a man who looks at his face in a mirror and, after looking at himself, goes away and immediately forgets what he looks like. But the man who looks intently into the perfect law that gives freedom, and continues to do this, not forgetting what he has heard, but doing it - he will be blessed in what he does' (Jas. 1:22-25)

Both Jesus and James then highlight the fruit of this process of building the practical application of the word of God into our lives: it sets us free, and we will be blessed in what we do (John 8:32, Jas. 1:25).

In the Potter's hands

'Like clay in the hand of the potter, so are you in my hand...'
(Jer. 18:6)

Clearly, as with the construction of any physical building, this building up of our Christian life in this way is a process which takes time. Learning is a conversation through life, and we grow through the ongoing dialogue between our understanding of the word of God and how it relates practically to different situations in life. It is this aspect of learning, growing and being formed through process which is brought out by Jeremiah's use of the motif of the clay and potter. The well-known words of Jeremiah 18:6, spoken to the ancient Israelites, highlight the **transformational nature of the word of God** in its effects upon us as we 'do our lives' with him. We are the clay in God's hands, while he is a potter who shapes and forms us.

It is God's intention to take our lives, and then change and transform us into becoming the people that he would have us to be, a people whom he can use to fulfil his kingdom purposes. He desires to make us into a holy nation and a kingdom of priests which he can use (1 Peter 2:5,9). These descriptions which Peter uses are not intended to be hyperbolic descriptions of people who have become believers but who remain ordinary and unchanged, rather they are expressive of the very intention of God for every one of us: *'...that you may declare the praises of him who called you out of darkness into his wonderful light'* (1 Peter 2:9).

It is clear from the Old Testament narrative that the ancient Israelites, or at least many of them, disliked being in the divine Potter's hands. With some notable exceptions, they generally wanted to live their lives like people in the surrounding nations, and they resisted the deep changes in their inward spiritual characters which doing daily life with God demanded of them, if they were not to be hindered in their walk with him. Witness their response to their varied experiences in the desert after the exodus from Egypt; their repeated compromises in the period of the Judges; their demand for a king in Samuel's time simply so that they could be like the surrounding nations, and then their succumbing to worshipping the gods of these nations as well, and so on. **The ancient Israelites never really grasped the fact of God's intention for them, vis. to transform them as people, knowing him in experience, so that they could fulfil his divine call upon their lives as his people, to make them into a nation of priests which could minister his word and truth to the surrounding peoples** (Ex. 19:5-6).

Although it is true that God does love us as we are, yet it is also true that **he cannot use us as we are to fulfil his purposes. He needs to change us and form us in order to use us**. This need for the transformation of our inward, spiritual characters is expressed in Scripture using several different metaphors: we are seen as clay in the divine Potter's hands (Jer. 18:6); we are to be made into sharpened swords or polished arrows for his use (Isa. 49:2); we are branches in the Vine which need to be pruned from time to time, so that we can become even more fruitful (John 15:1-8), and so on.

The transformation of our life comes about through the interaction of the teaching and kingdom principles of the word of God with our everyday experience of life. We learn, we grow and we change as we submit to learning to practise the principles of the word in the experience of our daily life as we too follow Jesus. The inward changes brought about in this way, form us into becoming the kind of people that God needs us to become in order to use us.

11

Although God does use our abilities in his work, yet it is our use-ability that he is really after. **Transformation brings increased use-ability**. As someone once said, if you are not willing for God to change you, then how on earth can you expect him to change anything (let alone the world) through you?

As I stated in the introduction, many of the chapters of this book deal with areas in which Christians can stumble or get hindered or even stuck in their growth. **The secret of continued growth and of overcoming in such areas is to learn how the word of God works in actual practice, and to be willing to undergo the sometimes difficult, but deeply transformational process which needs to happen in order for victory to come and for growth to continue.**

For example, in order to overcome hurts, wounds and inward bitterness which may have affected us deeply, we must learn to forgive and to actually do this, giving real, genuine and full forgiveness, and in this way free ourselves from the hold that the hurt has had upon us. As another example, the only way to learn to trust that God <u>will</u> provide, is to allow him to take us through a time of lack and learn the lesson of seeking first the kingdom of God and his righteousness, and then seeing him faithfully keep his promise of provision. Similarly, if we want to learn about God's healing power in practice, then we must learn to approach dealing with sickness in terms of biblical principles and promises rather than being dependant only on the medical profession. Again, if we would have spiritual victory in our lives, then we must learn how to fight in spiritual warfare whether we like it or not.

The lessons learnt by becoming willing to 'take the plunge,' as it were, and to actually learn to put biblical principles into practice as they pertain to various issues in life, mould us and fashion us inwardly, and bring about the transformation of our lives which causes growth to take place. Such inward transformation both frees us and takes us into new realms of being able to be used by the Master in the work of his kingdom. **These lessons of transformation ingrain the principles of the word of God indelibly within us, and hence they are keys to victory.**

2

THE MEANING OF THE CROSS

'For I resolved to know nothing while I was with you except Jesus Christ and him crucified' (1 Cor. 2:2)

'For the message of the cross is foolishness to those who are perishing, but to us who are being saved it is the power of God' (1 Cor. 1:18)

THE death of Jesus Christ on the cross is the heart of the Christian faith. The meaning of the cross, as explained below, gives rise to the basic nature of the Christian faith as being rooted in grace, mercy, forgiveness, love, and so on. Furthermore, Jesus' death on the cross is inseparable from his resurrection three days later; they are two sides of a single coin, together making a complete work of redemption. In resurrecting Jesus from the dead, God affirmed the work accomplished by his death on the cross (Rom. 1:4). So the resurrection of Jesus from the dead is also seen as the essential backbone of our faith (1 Cor. 15). Jesus conquered death and so, through this, we can also have victory over the fear of death.

Several truths ought to encourage us to develop a thorough understanding of the meaning of the cross, and thereby build and establish a strong foundation for our faith:

15

a. the fact that the cross deals thoroughly with the problem of human sin;

b. the fact that Jesus came in order to destroy the devil's work (1 John 3:8), that *'by his death [Jesus] might destroy him who holds the power of death – that is, the devil...'* (Heb. 2:14);

c. and the fact that this human fear of death has been dealt a fatal blow at its roots by the resurrection of Jesus Christ our Lord: *'...and free those who all their lives were held in slavery by their fear of death'* (Heb. 2:15).

A once for all atoning sacrifice for sin

The death of Jesus on the cross was an atoning sacrifice for human sin. He was the sacrificial *'Lamb of God who takes away the sin of the world'* (John 1:29). 'Atonement' is literally 'a making at one,' meaning therefore that the cross removes our sin and so deals with the estrangement between humankind and God, allowing us to be restored into right relationship with him.

Jesus' sacrifice of himself for us was a 'once for all' substitutionary sacrifice: it was done once, for all time (Heb. 10:12) and for all people (1 John 2:2). The Greek word *hapax* and its strengthened form *ephapax*, used several times in the epistle to the Hebrews and translated 'once' or 'once for all,' imply an act that is of perpetual validity which does not need to be repeated. **So the death of Jesus on the cross deals effectively, conclusively and totally with the problem of human sin**: *'he has appeared once for* *all at the end of the ages to do away with sin by the sacrifice of himself'* (Heb. 9:26).

In Adam, in Christ

Reading: Romans 5:12-21

The **key to understanding the work of Christ in gaining our salvation on the cross, is that Jesus the Son of God was our representative as the head of the redeemed community of faith.** In God's purpose, because Jesus is our representative head, all the benefits of his work of salvation are accounted to us, in just the same way that we inherited sin, death, condemnation and judgement as the consequences of Adam's fall into sin. **We partake in everything that Jesus gained through his work on the cross and his resurrection.** As non-believers, we were 'in Adam,' but now, as believers, we have been included 'in Christ' (Eph. 1:13). So, through living faith in him, we gain grace, justification, righteousness and eternal life, and so on (see Rom. 5:12-21). This is the meaning of the apostle Paul's statement that *'it is because of [God] that you are in Christ Jesus, who has become for us wisdom from God – that is, our righteousness, holiness and redemption'* (1 Cor. 1:30).

Hence, because Jesus is our new head, God reckons us as having died in Christ when he died on the cross, and that we therefore have died to sin (Rom. 6:2-4,6-8). We have been raised with Christ when he was raised from the dead, and have been given new spiritual life through him (Rom. 6:4-5,8-10; Eph. 1:19, 2:5), and we will also be raised physically from the dead when he returns for us (1 Cor. 15:21-23). Furthermore, we have also been raised up with Christ in his ascension and are seated with him in heavenly places (Eph. 2:6).

This all represents the fullness of the 'great salvation' that Jesus gained for us (Heb. 2:3). From being captives to sin and under the dominion of darkness, we have become servants and heirs of God, freed from sin and reigning in life through Christ.

Hence, because of this salvation in Christ, Paul argues that we should not let sin reign in our lives, but should give ourselves over to serving righteousness (Rom. 6:11-23), so that God's intention for us in our salvation is fulfilled. Being in Christ is also the basis of the deep, inward assurance that believers can know when facing death and bereavement (1 Thess. 4:13-18, 1 Cor. 15).

Propitiation

Sin provokes wrath in the one sinned against. This is true in human life, and it is also true that human sin and our enmity against God provoke his wrath. God's wrath is the settled opposition of his holy nature towards sin and evil. Hence, when people no longer consider it worthwhile to retain the knowledge of God, God, in his wrath, gives them over to the consequences of their sin (Rom. 1:18-32). To be consistent with his nature, therefore, God must condemn and judge sin. This is also true of law-breaking in the human realm. The judging of sin is the demonstration of God's justice (Rom. 3:25-26). **Sin merits judgement:** *'the wages of sin is death'* (Rom. 6:23). So, in order for us to know and experience the grace and forgiveness of God, this barrier of sin, wrath and judgement must first be overcome.

The word 'propitiation' is used in the New Testament to refer to the satisfying and removal of the wrath of God towards sin through the sacrifice of Jesus on the cross: *'Whom God hath set forth to be a propitiation through faith in his blood, to declare his righteousness for the remission of sins that are past...'* (Rom. 3:25 AV). 'Propitiation' translates the Greek word *hilasterion* which was used to describe the way in which the ancient Greeks would attempt to appease the wrath and secure the favour of their capricious gods by means of a sacrificial offering.

Propitiation is rooted in God's grace and his love for us: *'Herein is love, not that we loved God, but that he loved us, and sent his Son to be the propitiation for our sins'* (1 John 4:10 AV). In his grace, God himself took the initiative in overcoming the barrier of sin, by presenting Jesus his Son as the one whose sacrifice of himself on the cross is the propitiation for our sin, through his blood (Rom. 3:25, Heb. 2:17): **as our representative, Jesus bore the judgement of God on our sin, dying in our place, thus satisfying God's wrath.**

So, in Christ, therefore, God's wrath against sin is removed and God is free to demonstrate his grace, love, mercy, forgiveness, faithful care, and so on, towards us. **We can then experience this grace, forgiveness and care, rather than living in the fear that perhaps we continue to be objects of his wrath and judgement. God is not angry with us:** *'I will heal their waywardness and love them freely, for my anger has turned away from them'* (Hosea 14:4 and cf. Rom. 5:9). Furthermore, Jesus' sacrifice for us continues to be our propitiation whenever we may sin as believers (1 John 2:1-2), so, if we confess our sins, he is faithful and just to forgive us our sins and to cleanse us from all unrighteousness (1 John 1:9).

If teaching on propitiation is neglected or if this truth is not understood, this can lead to us having a lack of assurance of God's love for us, as we may believe that God is still angry with us or that we somehow have to earn his grace and love. No, Jesus did it all on the cross by removing God's wrath towards sin, by dying in our place. **God's wrath has been removed in Jesus**, and we have been freed to experience his grace and love.

Forgiveness

Forgiveness, both in human life and in regard to our relationship with God, presupposes an offence which needs to be pardoned. Closely related to it are the concepts of indebtedness and being released from the obligation to repay debt. Jesus made this clear in the parable of the unmerciful servant (see Matt. 18:21-35). Our sin, having caused offence towards God, makes us indebted to him and, of course, it is a debt that we are unable to repay, for *'the wages of sin is death'* (Rom. 6:23); sin merits only judgement. **However, it is God's mercy which is at the heart of his forgiveness of sin.**

In the Old Testament sacrificial system, forgiveness for sins came about through the shedding of the blood of an animal sacrifice. When the blood was sprinkled on the mercy-seat, God forgave the people, covered over their sins and took away their guilt (Lev. 16), making them outwardly clean (Heb. 9:13), although their inward consciences were not cleansed or freed (Heb. 10:2-4).

God forgives our sins because of the shedding of Christ's blood on the cross (Eph. 1:7; Heb. 9:12,14,22). **Through his death, Jesus covered and paid our debt.** The underlying meaning of the Greek words *aphesis* (meaning 'remission' and used for forgiveness) and *apoluo* (Luke 6:37) is that of being loosed or released from something, or of being sent away. God looses or releases us from our indebtedness to him and from judgement, and Christ's blood cleanses our hearts (Heb. 9:14,10:22) and frees us from our sin (1 John 1:7,9; Rev. 1:5b). God will remember our sins no more (Heb. 10:17). In Christ, they have been **expiated (cancelled, blotted out, erased), cleansed, removed and taken away**. Our slate has been wiped clean and we have been given a new start (cf. Ps. 51:1,9; Ps. 103:12; Isa. 1:18; Heb. 9:26): *'He has made perfect forever those who are being made holy'* (Heb. 10:14).

God's forgiveness is not something that we should take lightly: *'If you, O LORD, kept a record of sins, O Lord, who could stand? But with you there is forgiveness; therefore you are feared'* (Ps. 130:3-4). An appreciation of our indebtedness to God and of his forgiveness ought to bring about a change in the attitude of our heart and so move us to repentance and forsaking sin. Experiencing real repentance and the forgiveness of God **frees us from sin and cleanses our conscience from guilt** (Heb. 9:14, 10:22). The fruit of experiencing God's forgiveness is inward peace, joy, praise, love for God and a desire to serve him: he loves much, to whom much has been forgiven (Luke 7:47).

Also, as we grow in our faith, we should learn to imitate God by forgiving those who have hurt us or have sinned against us. We should forgive each other, just as in Christ God has forgiven us (Eph. 4:32 – 5:1; Matt. 5:43-48).

Redemption / Ransom

The truth of the forgiveness of sin is closely related to that of redemption: *'In [Christ] we have redemption through his blood, the forgiveness of sins...'* (Eph. 1:7 and cf. Col. 1:14). The concept of redemption centres on the issue of **ownership**. In the Old Testament, a person paid a price to re-possess land or property which they or their family had previously owned, but which in time had come into the possession of someone else. In Greek-Roman times, the word *agorazo* ('to buy' cf. 1 Cor. 6:20) was used of purchasing slaves from the market, and the word *lutron* (meaning 'ransom') was used to describe the price paid for prisoners-of-war that they might be released. In the New Testament, the word *apolutrosis* (translated as 'redemption') refers to the process of securing the freedom of something upon payment of a ransom-price (the *lutron*).

In the New Testament, the emphasis is placed both on the price paid for our redemption (i.e. the blood of Jesus) and on what has been purchased by that price (i.e. believers as a redeemed community). So redemption refers to God's act of intervention to deliver us from being captives to the power of sin. Jesus gave his life *'as a ransom for many'* (Mark 10:45). We have been redeemed with the price of the blood of Christ (Col. 1:14; 1 Tim. 2:5-6; 1 Peter 1:18-19), and we have become God's property (Eph. 1:14, 4:30). Our sins have been forgiven (Eph. 1:7, 1 Peter 1:18-19), and we are no longer captives to sin (cf. Rom. 6:17-18, 7:14) or to Satan's dominion, but we are owned by God. We have been rescued from the dominion of darkness and brought into the kingdom of God's Son (Col. 1:13). As his sheep, we have been marked out as belonging to God by being sealed with his seal of ownership, the Holy Spirit (Eph. 1:7,13-14) who is the guarantee of our future inheritance.

So, we have been **ransomed through the death of Jesus** (Mark 10:45), **redeemed by his blood** (Eph. 1:7, Heb. 9:12) and **bought with a price. We are not our own** (1 Cor. 6:19-20); *we belong to God.*

Reconciliation

In redeeming us, God did what was necessary to restore the ruptured relationship and estrangement between humankind and himself, reconciling us to himself: *'...that God was reconciling the world to himself in Christ, not counting men's sins against them...'* (2 Cor. 5:18-21). God does not need to be reconciled to us; it is we who are in need of being reconciled to him, as our sinful mind is naturally hostile towards God (Rom. 8:7). Through his grace, God has overcome this hostility: we were reconciled to him through the death of his Son Jesus when we were his enemies (Rom. 5:10; Eph. 2:16; Col. 1:22).

So, being redeemed and reconciled to God, **not only are we SAVED FROM sin, but we also have the privilege of being SAVED INTO a living relationship with God.** Instead of being estranged from and at enmity with him, we are now reconciled to and at peace with him (Col. 1:20). **The heart of what it means to be a Christian is about coming into a living covenant relationship with God**: *'I will be their God and they will be my people'* (Heb. 8:10). God desires that we develop this relationship with him as his beloved children (Rom. 8:15-17).

Furthermore, perhaps one of the clearest practical consequences of the truths of redemption and reconciliation, is **God's commitment to protect, provide for and care for his people**, for we are now his treasured possession (cf. Mal. 3:17). God redeems us in order to reconcile us to himself in **a covenant relationship,** and hence this is a relationship to which he is committed in terms of his care, protection and provision for us. So, having now been reconciled to him, how much more shall we be saved through Christ's life! (Rom.

5:10). **This should give us deep assurance as we learn to trust him in our lives.**

Justification

The apostle Paul's famous rhetorical question: *'If God is for us, who can be against us?'* (Rom. 8:31) expresses the triumphant confidence which a believer experiences when s/he is living in the assurance that s/he is justified before God.

Jesus, as our representative before God, perfectly fulfilled the demands of the Law for us. He took the judgement of God upon himself on the cross (Rom. 3:25), with our sin being accounted to him (taking our sin upon himself and becoming sin for us, 2 Cor. 5:21), and so God, in his grace and mercy, pardons our sin and accepts us when we receive Jesus by faith. However, justification is more than simply being acquitted of our guilt and pardoned so that we are no longer condemned as a result of our sin. As our representative, his completed and perfect work for us was affirmed through his resurrection (Rom. 1:4), and his own perfect righteousness is then accounted to us, through our faith. We are, therefore, justified by his blood and through his resurrection (Rom. 4:25, 5:9), so we can be fully reconciled to God and enter into peace with him (Rom. 5:1).

So God's verdict is that, in Christ, we are declared, accepted and treated by God as being perfectly righteous: *'God made him who had no sin to be sin for us, so that in him we might become the righteousness of God'* (2 Cor. 5:21; and see Rom. 3:24; 4:3-8; 5:15-21; 1 Cor. 1:30). **Hence, when God sees us, he sees us as we are in Christ: *perfect.*** Clearly, this is the free gift of God's grace to us

(Rom. 3:24, Titus 3:7), and comes as a result of believing the gospel and receiving Jesus. We do not deserve it and we cannot earn it by living a religious life or by doing good works (Rom. 4:16,24; 5:1; 10:4). Being justified in this way gives us access to God's blessings and to his favour as his children.

This truth gives us great confidence when we are tempted to doubt perhaps because of personal failures and weaknesses, or because the enemy of our souls is plaguing us with doubts. In Christ, God has freely and fully justified us, so therefore *'there is now no condemnation for those who are in Christ Jesus'* (Rom. 8:1). Our guilt has been taken away, our sin has been forgiven and we stand washed clean and clothed in a new robe of Christ's righteousness (Rev. 7:14). So, as Paul continued: *'Who will bring any charge against those whom God has chosen?... Who is he who condemns?... It is God who justifies'* (Rom. 8:33-34).

It is very important for us as believers to realise that we do not ever have to try to get into a position of 'no condemnation' before God by trying to sin less or by trying to live better. No, from the very beginning of our walk with him God declares that we stand in the truth of 'no condemnation' before him, and it is standing on the ground of this truth that we are then empowered to sin less and can cast down any accusations or doubts from the devil in our minds.

Adoption

Another important metaphor used in the New Testament, and which follows on as a result of justification, is that of **our adoption as children of God.** The Greek word *huiothesia* transliterates as 'to be placed as a son' and means that, having been justified by God and brought into relationship with him, we are placed into the family / household of God as his children (Gal. 4:5-6, Eph. 1:5, Heb. 3:6). The word refers to the Roman practice of the adoption of children into a family, whereby they received the same legal and inheritance rights as sons born naturally into that family (Rom. 8:15-17).

So, in adoption, **God becomes our Father and we are his children**, living in covenant relationship with him (2 Cor. 6:16-18). This is a right belonging to all those who believe in Jesus: *'Yet to all who received him, to those who believed in his name, he gave the right to become children of God...'* (John 1:12-13). Jesus is therefore our elder brother in God's family, the firstborn among us as his brethren (Rom. 8:29), and, as a consequence, we are also joint-heirs with Christ in his kingdom (Rom. 8:17). Together, we make up God's redeemed community. The Holy Spirit within us bears witness with our spirits that God is our Father and that we are his children, and, as we grow in our faith, we can then develop confidence and intimacy in this personal relationship we have with him (Rom. 8:15-16, Gal. 4:6).

'For you did not receive a spirit that makes you a slave again to fear, but you received the Spirit of adoption. And by him we cry, "Abba, Father." The Spirit himself testifies with our spirit that we are God's children. Now if we are children, then we are heirs – heirs of God and co-heirs with Christ, if indeed we share in his sufferings in order that we may also share in his glory' (Rom. 8:15-17)

Regeneration / Renewal

When a person genuinely receives Jesus and repents from their old life, s/he is **born again**. This is a metaphor used to describe the internal, spiritual work which is done within us by the Holy Spirit whereby he brings us into a state of regenerated and renewed spiritual life. Before we received Jesus, we were separated from the life of God, and so we were spiritually *'dead in transgressions and sins,'* but now we have been *'made alive with Christ'* (Eph. 2:1,4). God acts in his grace, mercy, love and kindness to bring us into this state of new spiritual life (Eph. 2:4-5).

Becoming born again happens to a person when they hear and receive the seed of the gospel, the word of truth:

'He chose to give us birth through the word of truth, that we might be a kind of firstfruits of all he created' (see Jas. 1:18,21)

'For you have been born again, not of perishable seed, but of imperishable, through the living and enduring word of God' (see 1 Peter 1:23 - 2:2)

The living seed of the word of the gospel is planted within us through hearing the message (Luke 8:11, Rom. 10:17), and new spiritual life is then birthed within us from this seed by the Holy Spirit (Titus 3:5) as we respond to the gospel in faith.

This is a definite, personal experience of internal spiritual regeneration. In Titus 3:5, Paul says that *'[God] saved us through the washing of rebirth and renewal by the Holy Spirit.'* So being born again is likened to **an internal spiritual washing through the word of God** (cf. Eph. 5:26). The Greek word *palingenesia* (meaning 'regeneration' or 'rebirth') is used elsewhere in the Scriptures in the context of **Messianic restoration** (Matt. 19:28). The Greek word *anakainosis* (translated 'renewal' and meaning 'to make something new') refers to the fact that this work of the Holy Spirit deep within us 'makes us new.' This word is used also in

Romans 12:2 of the renewing of our minds. So it is not that God merely renovates our old life, rather he does away with it and replaces it with a new life in Christ, empowered within us by his Spirit.

This experience of being born again is also likened to **becoming a new creation** (2 Cor. 5:17, Gal. 6:15) and to **being spiritually resurrected with Christ** (Eph. 2:5). When we are born again we become God's children (John 1:12-13) and members of his kingdom (John 3:3,5; Col. 1:13).

So being born again brings us into a new spiritual life in which we experience the presence, life and power of God within us (John 3:3-8, Col. 3:4), freeing us from the power of habitual sin (1 John 3:9, 5:18). As this new life germinates and grows within us, it begins to produce the life of Christ in us (Col. 1:27) and **makes us into new people** (2 Cor. 5:17, Eph. 4:24, Col. 3:10). Our old life has passed away.

The new covenant

The underlying meaning of the Hebrew word *berith* (used in the Old Testament for 'covenant') emphasized **the mutual bond** between two parties in a covenant relationship. So God gave himself unreservedly to his people, and they in turn gave themselves to him and belonged to him. Hence his oft-repeated promise to them: *'I will be their God, and they will be my people.'* However, although the old Mosaic covenant (which was based on law, rules and regulations) was good in itself (Rom. 7:12), yet it did not have the power to change people internally in their hearts. It led the Israelites into powerless, religious living which was unable to help them to overcome the sinful nature within them (Rom. 7:7-25), and their track record was generally one of unfaithfulness towards God (Heb. 8:7-9). So God, through Jeremiah, **promised a new covenant which would succeed where the old one had failed,** and this new covenant is fulfilled in Jesus (Jer. 31:31-34, Heb. 8:8-12, 2 Cor. 3:6-11).

This new covenant is <u>not</u> a contract (the Greek word *syntheke*) between believers on the one part and God on the other, in which both parties agree to undertake mutual obligations towards one another, as if they are equals. The Greek word used in the New Testament for 'covenant' is *diatheke* which was used in everyday life to refer to the disposition of property through a will, and this is the way in which it is used in Hebrews 9:15-18. So it expresses the purpose stated by the one party making the will, rather than the idea of mutual obligations. Hence, the concept of covenant in the New Testament describes the will of the one Person, God, for us, in Christ, and this came into effect upon the death of Jesus.[1]

This new covenant then is an undertaking by God to bring us to himself through the cross and to bind us to himself as his people, in Christ (2 Cor. 6:16), **with all the benefits and the eternal inheritance that this then brings to us as his people** (Heb. 9:15). Jesus, as the mediator, is the guarantor of this new covenant (Heb. 7:22, 9:15). A person can accept this will of God for him/herself (through faith in Jesus), or s/he can reject it (by rejecting the message of the gospel). However, the purpose and intention of God for us in Christ, expressed in this *diatheke*, cannot be changed or altered any more than the terms of a person's will can be altered after the person has died. When a person has received Jesus, s/he can then

---

[1] See Archer, G.L. "Covenant" in *Baker's Dictionary of Theology* (Ed. Hamilton, E.F.), London: Pickering and Inglis, 1960, pp.142-144.

enter into the full provisions of this will of God for them. So we enter this new covenant relationship with God through the blood of Jesus which was shed for the forgiveness, cleansing and taking away of our sins (Matt. 26:28, Rom. 11:27, 1 Cor. 11:25, Heb. 13:20).

The variety of motifs which are described in the sections above in this chapter, are descriptive of this new covenant. So, in this covenant, God redeems and reconciles us to himself, binding himself to us in relationship through Christ, and promises that he will give us a new heart and a new spirit, making us into new people, placing his Spirit in our hearts to empower our spiritual lives (Ezek. 36:26-27; Eph. 1:13-14; 2 Cor. 3:6,17-18). The indwelling Holy Spirit will then move us to follow his decrees and keep his laws (Ezek. 36:27) which will be written on our hearts (Heb. 8:10, 10:16). This gives us an inclination and desire within ourselves to live with him and for him according to his word. **We will know God and walk with him in a true, loving filial relationship as his children by his Spirit**, rather than simply knowing <u>about</u> him (Heb. 8:11). It is a covenant relationship in which God has promised that he will dwell in and among his people by his Spirit's presence: *'I will live with them and walk among them, and I will be their God, and they will be my people'* (2 Cor. 6:16, 1 Cor. 3:16).

Our identity in Christ

From the meaning of the cross as explained above, we can summarize some basic truths that help towards forming our **identity in Christ.** It is very important – even crucial! – that we understand these, in order that we can then take our stand on them, particularly in times when our minds are perhaps plagued by doubts or when the enemy of our souls attacks our minds with lies or insinuations about

God's character or the complete nature of the work that Jesus did for us on the cross.

a. God sees me as being in Christ. Jesus is my head, my Lord and my king. All the benefits of his salvation have been accounted to me; they are mine.

b. God is not angry towards me because of my sins. He is gracious to me and loves me. Jesus took the judgement for my sin when he died on the cross.

c. I have been bought with the blood of Jesus. In Christ, I died to sin and I am no longer captive to it; sin will not have dominion over me. I am no longer under the dominion of darkness. The devil was defeated and destroyed at the cross. I belong to God. I am in his kingdom.

d. I am God's property and have been sealed as such by the abiding presence of the Holy Spirit in my life. I do not belong to the devil. He who is within me is greater than he who is in the world (1 John 4:4).

e. I am forgiven. The blood of Jesus Christ cleanses me from ALL sin. I have been freed from the power of habitual sin.

f. God has made me perfectly righteous in his sight. He is FOR me, not against me, and no accusing voices carry any weight before him.

g. God is my Father and I belong to him. I have been adopted by him and am a member of his household. My Father is committed to me and will care for me, provide for me and protect me.

h. I am a born-again child of God. I have the presence, life and power of God within me.

i. I died with Christ and have been raised with him. I am seated in heavenly places in him. I am an heir of God, a joint-heir with Christ. I will reign in life through Christ.

j. I am bound to God in covenant relationship. I will receive a promised eternal inheritance. He is committed to me and dwells within me by his Spirit.

3

REPENTANCE

'The kingdom of God is near. Repent and believe the good news!'
(Mark 1:15)

'Nevertheless, God's solid foundation stands firm, sealed with this inscription: "The Lord knows those who are his," and, "Everyone who confesses the name of the Lord must depart from iniquity."'
(2 Tim. 2:19)

A positive and powerful concept

TOGETHER with faith in God, **repentance is one of the two foundational keys in genuine conversion to the Christian life and to continuing to walk with God in a life of obedience and submission to him.**

This primary need for repentance was emphasized by John the Baptist (Matt. 3:1-2), by Jesus (Mark 1:15 above) and by the apostle Peter: *'Repent and be baptized, every one of you, in the name of Jesus Christ for the forgiveness of your sins'* (Acts 2:38). It is inferred as being foundational in 2 Timothy 2:19 (above) and, in Hebrews 6:1-2, repentance is the first of the several foundational teachings mentioned: *'Therefore let us... go on to maturity, not laying again <u>the foundation of repentance</u>...'* (Heb. 6:1, underlining my own for emphasis).

Repentance has two essential elements. Firstly, turning away from and forsaking sin, and, secondly, turning toward God with faith in the Lord Jesus Christ: *'turn to God in repentance and have faith in our Lord Jesus Christ'* (Acts 20:21). We repent <u>from</u> sin and <u>turn toward</u> God, on the basis of what Jesus did for us, bearing our sins on the cross and making it possible for us to have a new life in him.

Since repentance involves turning away from sin and the problems and bondage that it causes, into a life of freedom from habitual sin, and also involves entering into a relationship with God with all the blessings of salvation that this can bring us, **repentance is seen biblically as a very positive and powerful concept.** It is God's patience and kindness which leads us to it (Acts 11:18, Romans 2:4, 2 Peter 3:9). Indeed, as Jesus repeatedly said, the angels of heaven rejoice over one sinner who repents (Luke 15:7,10).

Repentance involves the whole person

Repentance involves the whole person and this is typified in the Parable of the Lost Son in Luke 15:11-32.

Reading: Luke 15:11-32

a. *Repentance involves our mind*

The Greek word used for repentance in the New Testament is *metanoia* which literally means to 'perceive afterwards' and so implies a change in the way in which we think about something, specifically in regard to sin and the way in which we live our lives. So **repentance is essentially coming to think about things and look upon them the way God sees and thinks about them from his perspective.** We realise that he is right and that our own way has been wrong. We repent when we get to the point where we can see that we have been wrong and we desire to change, when we get to the point where we no longer want sin (or a particular sin) in our lives, and when we no longer want to stay as we are or to continue on in our own ways in our present lifestyle.

b. *Repentance involves our conscience*

Luke tells us that the lost son *'came to his senses'* (Luke 15:17). After the wayward manner in which he had lived his life, he finally came to his right mind. He became aware in his conscience that he had sinned both against God and against his own father: *'I have sinned...'* (Luke 15:18). This conscious awareness then created sorrow in his heart.

c. *Repentance involves our heart*

Our hearts express repentance as sorrow for sin: *'your sorrow led you to repentance... Godly sorrow brings repentance that leads to salvation'* (2 Cor. 7:9-10). When the lost son returned to his father, he said to him, *'I have sinned against heaven and against you. I am no longer worthy to be called your son...'* (Luke 15:18-19).

d. *Repentance involves our will and leads us to action*

Words, feelings and thoughts were not enough for the lost son. He said to himself, *'I will set out and go back to my father'* (Luke 15:18). He got up and did something about his sin and broken lifestyle. **Repentance moved him to go and confess his wrong, and to put a broken relationship right.**

35

e. *So repentance involves a change of direction: turning around and walking in a new direction*

This is the essence of the Greek word *epistrepho*, used in Acts 11:21 where it says that *'a great number of people believed and turned to the Lord.'* It literally means to turn around and face the other way, implying a decisive act as a consequence of a deliberate choice. So it says of the lost son that he *'got up and went'* (Luke 15:20), forsaking his sin and turning his back on his broken lifestyle.

Believing but not repenting?

'The Christ will suffer and rise from the dead on the third day, and repentance and forgiveness of sins will be preached in his name to all nations' (Luke 24:46-47)

To neglect to preach about repentance is tantamount to preaching only half a gospel, and in fact it is no gospel at all. People who respond to a message which involves believing in Jesus, but which is weak on the element of repentance, may well continue to struggle with sinful habits in their personal lives until they understand their need to forsake sins they become consciously aware of. **If we really do want to have victory over sin in our lives, then our primary need is to repent of sin and to forsake it and any lifestyle habits associated with it.**

So it should be no surprise that, in a church which is weak on teaching and practising repentance, we might find people who are still struggling with basic sins or issues, sinful attitudes and/or unrestored relationships in their lives.

Paul reminded the believers in the church in Corinth about the importance of repentance, when he rebuked them for the sins and behaviour that were wrecking the life of their church. He told them not to deceive themselves in this regard – people who do not repent from their sinful lifestyles will not inherit the kingdom of God (1 Cor. 6:9-10). At the end of two long letters to them, he challenged them to *'Examine yourselves to see whether you are in the faith; test yourselves. Do you not realize that Christ Jesus is in you – unless, of course, you fail the test?'* (2 Cor. 13:5). For Paul, if Christ really was living in a person, then this ought to issue forth in real-life repentance from sin.

In our own day, neglecting or not having the courage to teach on repentance may perhaps be pandering to political correctness or to the fear of people's response to the message of repentance, but such neglect betrays a root of lack of God's love for people. Because God loves people, they should hear – and have the right to hear, and indeed need to hear – teaching on repentance. The love of God is firm – believe AND repent. **It is repentance that leads a person into true freedom.**

So repent and live the life that God wants you to have

a. **All people everywhere are commanded by God to repent** (Acts 17:30), but it is also an exhortation and an invitation by him. This is because, in the work of Jesus on the cross, God has done what is needed to bring people out of the spiritual darkness and bondage to sin in which they live, into the blessings of life in his kingdom – there is no need for people to remain in their present state anymore, and the way is open into his kingdom.

Jesus took our sin upon himself, so we do not need to carry on in it any longer! God yearns for us to know him and his life and blessings, so he commands, exhorts and invites us to do what we need to do, to take this step and repent.

b. Repentance not only means accepting Jesus as our personal Saviour, but also recognizing him as the Lord and Master of our life. It involves submission to him and surrendering our life to him, so that we can follow him. It means learning to know the word of God and aligning our lifestyle and choices to reflect a true understanding of the word of God in practice.

c. If the Christian life can be likened to a race (see 1 Cor. 9:24-27, 1 Tim. 2:5, Heb. 12:1), then **repentance from sin represents the starting line of this race, not simply a hurdle that we face for the first time somewhere further round the track.**

Furthermore, rather than being something that we do only at the beginning of our Christian lives, repentance is an ongoing and integral part of the Christian life, and, without it, it is impossible to experience the full blessings of the kingdom of God. The believers in no less than five out of the seven churches mentioned in Revelation 2-3 were exhorted to repent (see Rev. 2:5, 2:16, 2:21; 3:3, 3:19).

Repentance is the key to living a clean life, free from sin. Repentant attitudes should characterize our lives in an ongoing way. Repentance involves becoming consciously aware of sin in our lives, confession of this sin (1 John 1:7-9) and a desire to turn away from it and to get it out of our lives. **To live a life of**

true freedom in Christ, the practice of repentance needs to become deep, thorough and ongoing.

Repentance, rejoicing and refreshing

God loves and delights to live with his people, and to manifest his presence amongst us, and repentance is the key to experiencing this blessing.

When the prodigal returned and was reconciled to his father, his father not only accepted and embraced his son, he also demonstrated his joy in their renewed relationship by having a feast and celebrating that *'the lost was now found.'* He put a new robe on his son, a ring on his finger and sandals on his feet, and killed the fattened calf to feast and celebrate (Luke 15:22-24). **This is a picture of God's extravagant grace towards us.** There is rejoicing in heaven over just one sinner who repents! (Luke 15:7).

The apostle Peter outlined the link between repentance and the empowering and refreshing presence of the Holy Spirit being poured out upon us: *'Repent and be baptized... for the forgiveness of your sins. **And you will receive the gift of the Holy Spirit'*** (Acts 2:38), and, *'Repent, then, and turn to God, so that your sins may be wiped out, **that times of refreshing may come from the Lord...'*** (Acts 3:19).

Such an experience of the manifest refreshing presence and power of the Holy Spirit is the covenant promise of God to all his people who live in repentance: *'I will live with them and walk among them, and I will be their God, and they will be my people'* (2 Cor.

6:16). This experience of a renewed spiritual life with the freedom, joy, praise and power of God's presence that comes with it, was the ongoing experience of the early church in the book of Acts, and it can be our experience too! **It is the life into which repentance brings us.**

4

BROKENNESS AND RESTORATION

'I have seen his ways, but I will heal him; I will guide him and restore comfort to him...' (Isa. 57:18)

'O afflicted city, lashed by storms and not comforted, I will build you with stones of turquoise, your foundations with sapphires' (Isa. 54:11)

Brokenness in society

THE lives of simply too many people today amply reflect the description in the verse above from Isaiah 54:11 – *afflicted, lashed by storms, not comforted.* The practical and social consequences of a philosophy, in which the existence of God is either denied altogether or conveniently laid aside as being irrelevant, ignored and then forgotten about, are stark. The Bible says that *'My people are destroyed from lack of knowledge'* (Hosea 4:6), and that it is the fool who says in his heart, *'There is no God'* (Ps. 14:1). Some of the destructive practical consequences of this erroneous belief are outlined to us in Psalms 14:1-3, 53:1-3 and Romans 1:18-32.

The brokenness and fragmentation brought about by secular atheism, in which the commandments, wisdom and promises of God are laid aside, have been commented upon by many writers today[2] and are clear to those who have eyes to see: *'Where there is no revelation, men cast off restraint'* (Prov. 29:18), and every person does *'that which [is] right in his own eyes'* (Judges 21:25 AV).

Our embrace of self-centred, godless individualism has had many consequences: materialism and greed for short-term financial gain, ingraining a depth of selfishness in people which has minimized the importance of relationships in general and the need for community, often regarding other people as valueless; a hedonistic and often shameless pursuit of selfish pleasure which ultimately fails to satisfy the human heart; a breakdown in the ability to sustain long-term relationships, with seemingly ever-higher degrees of stress, betrayal within marriage, spiralling divorce rates (and multiple divorces), broken and dysfunctional families, the wound of fatherlessness for far too many children, and intergenerational divorce patterns; increased isolation, loneliness, suspicion, fear and the unwillingness to show genuine care, and so on.

This brokenness and fragmentation in society is often accompanied by deep, inner loneliness, emptiness, heart wounds and cynicism. Often symptomatic of these are such things as feelings of meaninglessness in life; binge drinking and alcoholism; comfort eating, gluttony and obesity; pornography, sexual promiscuity with its resultant STDs and unwanted pregnancies; waywardness and drug addiction; anger and violence in society, and despair leading to suicide, and so on. Too many people are deeply hurt by life. Thrown around, wearied and without hope, atheism offers them little

---

[2] For example, see Kirk, J.A. *OTC308 Mission Theology in Context*, Cheltenham: OTC, 2007, p.35.

or no healing for their wounds; their inward heart cry goes unheard. **Brokenness is a common experience.**

This heart cry of meaninglessness, inward emptiness, hopelessness and despair, was echoed repeatedly by the writer of Ecclesiastes: *'Utterly meaningless! Everything is meaningless'* (Eccl. 1:2 etc.). And what was his conclusion? *'Remember your Creator in the days of your youth...'* (Eccl. 12:1). True and lasting meaningfulness in life is found only through being restored into a right relationship with God, which will then lead us into rightly relating to ourselves and to people around us.

Restoration to wholeness is God's purpose

One of the central motifs given to us in Scripture of the salvation of God is that of **restoration.** In a word, where there has been brokenness, he can restore and rebuild. Just as he did for ancient Israel after a period of brokenness in their national life, he can *'rebuild the ancient ruins and restore the places long devastated'* in our lives (Isa. 61:4). He can take afflicted lives which have been lashed by storms and not comforted, and rebuild them with stones of turquoise and their foundations with sapphires (Isa. 54:11). His thoughts and plans for us are to prosper us and not to harm us, to give us hope and a future (Jer. 29:11). He satisfies the longing soul (Ps. 107:9 AV). On the very points where Satan (the thief) has stolen from, killed and destroyed us, Jesus can give us abundant life to the full (John 10:10), so restoring the intention of God for our lives.

There is a very real sense in which rebuilding and restoring broken lives is God's speciality. He is a God of hope (Rom. 15:13) and he yearns to bring this living hope into our lives. **The gospel is**

good news. If our lives have been characterized by brokenness in any way, then, in Jesus, **the healing and restoration of that brokenness is our living hope.**

To describe this hope, the Old Testament often uses the words *yasha* ('to save' or 'to deliver,' and literally meaning to bring someone out of a restricted place into an open and free place, cf. Ps. 18:19, 118:5) and *shalom* (describing the general state of well-being and wholeness into which God brings people). Similarly, the New Testament uses the words *sozo* ('to save') and *soteria* ('salvation') to refer to the deliverance we experience in Christ (being saved from sin, or delivered out of one state of being and life, into another, and also used to sum up all the blessings bestowed by God on his people in Christ). So **the salvation to which the Bible refers speaks of a restored life, restored relationships and wholeness, in the context of belonging to the kingdom of God** (Col. 1:13-14).

Jesus rebuilds broken lives

Jesus came into a broken, frustrated world and offered people the good news of the kingdom of God. By his acts of grace for people, he demonstrated the fact that God cares for the whole of our lives in every aspect. To come into the kingdom of God through Jesus, means that we can progressively come to know and experience his caring authority over the whole of our life. So he brought – and still brings! – good news to the poor; he binds up the broken-hearted; he gives freedom to the captive; he comforts those who mourn and provides for those who grieve; he bestows on them a crown of beauty instead of ashes, the oil of gladness instead of mourning, a garment of praise instead of a spirit of despair, making

44

them into oaks of righteousness and a people who can then display his splendour to others around (Isa. 61:1-3, Luke 4:18-19).

Jesus' ministry was characterized by bringing grace and forgiveness to those who would repent. He acted to bring God's salvation into different situations and needs in people's lives (such as healing the sick, freeing those who were oppressed and enslaved by evil spirits, and cleansing lepers). He brought healing to broken relationships. He ministered to those who were marginalized, to the poor, to those who were suffering and to the weak. He reached out to widows, to women, to children and orphans; to the broken-hearted, to those who mourned and grieved, to the despairing; to prostitutes, tax collectors and so-called 'sinners.' He was a compassionate shepherd to the harassed and helpless sheep of his people: **he took the lives of poor, broken, neglected and despised people, restored them and put them on their feet again.** He took away the deep frustration and brokenness of their lives and brought them into the glorious blessing and freedom of the children of God (Rom. 8:20-21).

Examples of restored lives

The gospel narratives contain many examples of people with broken lives. These are given to us by the writers as specific examples of the power of Jesus to transform people's lives for good as they experience his salvation. We can see that such brokenness manifested itself in different ways in the lives of the people we read about, and we can see how Jesus restored them.

As a consequence of his wilfulness and profligate living, the prodigal was eventually left penniless, friendless, homeless, and

45

without dignity, and, in his desperation and hunger, was forced to do any kind of work, even work he hated doing, just in order to survive. **Humbled and broken; barefoot, hungry and in rags!** But how did his father respond when he repented and returned home? He had deep compassion on him and received him back into his house (speaking of being received into the kingdom of God); he put the best robe on him (speaking of the righteousness of Christ, a new standing and identity as a child of God); he put a ring on his finger (speaking of receiving the Holy Spirit); he put sandals on his feet (speaking of a new commission to preach the message of God's kingdom to others); he killed the fattened calf, and the family rejoiced together in a great feast (Luke 15:20-24). **Restored!**

There were people whose lives had been devastated by broken health for years. The woman with the issue of blood is a well-known example (Luke 8:43-48). She was incurable, having suffered and being progressively weakened more and more by this debilitating condition for twelve long years, and she had also become impoverished by spending all her money on medical bills, only to find that the doctors could not cure her condition anyway. **Sick, desperate and becoming increasingly poor: broken and seemingly without hope!** But someone told her about Jesus (Mark 5:27) and hope rose up in her heart. She set off and went to Jesus, pushing her way through the crowd to reach him. When she took hold of the hem of his garment by faith, the power of God shot through her body and she was healed instantly and completely. **Restored!**

Then again there was the woman who had lived with five different husbands and was now with a sixth man. She was probably barren and not able to have children, looking for love and committed faithfulness, but not finding it. So she ended up effectively being passed around from one man to another, each separating from her after a short time together because she could not produce a son for them. **No commitment to her, no compassion, no care, just selfishness, using her and then casting her aside to be used by yet other men, leaving her a broken woman on the scrap heap of life.** What did Jesus do? He promised her a fountain of living water which would rise up from within her to heal and satisfy her broken heart completely. **Through this encounter with Jesus she was transformed** and many of the people in her town also became believers! (John 4:7-18,28-29,39-42).

The journey into wholeness

The kinds of things that are described above were only the beginning of these people's journey into wholeness, and there are many other examples in Scripture of God's restoring power in people's lives. As we ourselves learn to walk with Jesus in our lives, seeking first God's kingdom, knowing his presence daily and empowered by the Holy Spirit within us, and as we learn to live according to his commandments, wisdom and promises, we too will experience his goodness, his restoring care and his salvation in every aspect of our lives. **This is his will and desire for every one of us.**

If you are aware of any particular areas of brokenness in your life (perhaps one of those areas mentioned above, or another which is not mentioned), know that it is his desire to bind up your wounds, and to heal and restore comfort to you and make you whole again. Open up yourself to him in prayer even as you read this today, and ask him to begin to heal and restore your area of brokenness. As you continue to pray your prayer for restoration, he will surely keep his promise to you and make you whole again!

5

BE FILLED WITH THE HOLY SPIRIT

'You will receive power when the Holy Spirit comes upon you; and you will be my witnesses...' (Acts 1:8)

'All of them were filled with the Holy Spirit and began to speak in other tongues as the Spirit enabled them' (Acts 2:4)

The Holy Spirit: God's life-giving and empowering dynamic

JESUS promised his disciples that, after his ascension and exaltation, he would send them another Comforter – a Person like himself – to take his place, the Holy Spirit. He said that the Holy Spirit would come and live within believers forever, and that he would convict the world of its sin of unbelief, about truth concerning himself (Jesus) and about the truth of Satan being judged. He also said that the Holy Spirit would remind believers of the things that Jesus had taught, would lead them into all truth and would show them things to come (see John 14:16,26; 15:26; 16:7-11,13).

The apostle Peter affirmed that **the coming of this inner presence of the Holy Spirit is the Father's promise to everyone without exception who repents and receives Jesus into their lives**:

49

'And you will receive the gift of the Holy Spirit. The promise is for you and your children and for all who are far off – for all whom the Lord our God will call' (Acts 2:38-39). So the Holy Spirit is the seal of God's covenant with all believers (Eph. 1:13). He will give us a new heart and a new spirit, and he will move us to desire to follow God's word (Ezek. 36:26-27).

The Church: God's charismatic community

This means that it is – and always has been – God's purpose that **his Church should be a community of people characterized by the powerful presence of the Holy Spirit**. It was the pouring out of the Holy Spirit on the early disciples that gave birth to this new, charismatic community of believers (see Acts 2).

Several motifs are used of the Holy Spirit in Scripture, including **fire; a gentle dove; fresh, flowing water**, and **a moving breeze of air**. It is the presence and power of this Person, the Holy Spirit, in such ways that makes all the difference in church life and meetings. Instead of formal and lifeless meetings, there is a life-giving presence which empowers, sets free and uplifts. The presence and power of the Holy Spirit **inspires faith and empowers spiritual life**. So church is not meant to be a lifeless, cold, religious and irrelevant place, but rather a place filled and animated by the pervasive presence of the Holy Spirit in and amongst believers. The apostle Paul underlined this when he wrote that **ministry in the life of the church is the ministry of the life-giving Spirit** (2 Cor. 4:3,6,8), rather than mere religious formality. We are to be *'a dwelling in which God lives by his Spirit'* (Eph. 2:22).

Marks of a Spirit-filled life and ministry

The New Testament narrative and epistles give us many examples and marks of what it means to live a Spirit-filled life and to be Spirit-empowered in ministry.

a. Perhaps the most significant consequence of the Holy Spirit's presence in our lives, is that he gives us **a deep, lasting, inward assurance and confidence that God has accepted us and made us his children**: *'For you did not receive a spirit that makes you a slave again to fear, but you received the Spirit of sonship. And by him we cry, "Abba, Father." The Spirit himself testifies with our spirit that we are God's children'* (Rom. 8:14-15).

b. Along with this, the effect of the presence and working of the Holy Spirit in a believer's life is that **the person's life and character is progressively being transformed from within, morally and spiritually, as Christ is formed within them** (Gal. 4:19, Col. 1:27). In place of the sin, bondage, shame and issues that characterized the person's life before, now there is a growth of the grace and fruit of the Spirit's life within them: *'love, joy, peace, patience, kindness, goodness, faithfulness, gentleness and self-control'* (Gal. 5:22-23). The enslaving power of sin loses its grip, and the person's inner life is animated with the life and power of God. **This transforming of character is powerfully effected from within a believer.** For example, Luke said that great grace and willing generosity with one another characterized the community life of the early believers (Acts 2:33-35).

c. Jesus underlined that one of the main reasons why believers need to live a Spirit-filled life is **so that they can be spiritually empowered, both for life and ministry:** *'you will receive power when the Holy Spirit has come upon you'* (Acts 1:8). This dynamic of spiritual power makes a big difference to the effectiveness of Christian life and ministry. The aims of Christian ministry are <u>supposed</u> to be accomplished not just by preaching words, but also with *'demonstration of the Spirit's power'* (1 Cor. 2:4). Jesus himself similarly ministered *'in the power of the Spirit'* (Luke 4:14,18-19).

It was this anointed power that enabled the early apostles to boldly preach the message of the cross, resurrection and exaltation of Jesus and also to be used to bring healing and freedom from oppression to those in need of these and, as a result, they *'turned the world upside down'* (Acts 17:6). Prayer meetings among the early believers were powerful (Acts 4:31) and they went everywhere preaching the word of God with great effect (Acts 8:4, 19:10).

d. So **boldness to preach the word of God** is also a mark of believers who are empowered by the Holy Spirit: *'they were all filled with the Holy Spirit and spoke the word of God boldly'* (Acts 4:31). Before the early disciples were filled with the Holy Spirit, they locked themselves behind closed doors out of fear of being persecuted (John 20:19). However, *'God did not give us a spirit of timidity, but a spirit of power, of love and of self-discipline'* (2 Tim. 1:7). The infilling of the Holy Spirit takes the fear of other people away from us! When Peter preached after he had been filled with the Holy Spirit, those who heard him were *'cut to the heart'* and many were converted (Acts 2:37,41).

e. The **free flow of inspired, passionate, joyful praise** is another of the evident marks of a Spirit-filled life: *'For they heard them speaking in tongues and praising God'* (Acts 10:46, 13:52; Luke 1:64). Jesus said that streams of living water would flow out from within us (John 7:37-39), and free, open praise in meetings is one way in which this manifests itself. *'Be filled with the Spirit. Speak to one another with psalms, hymns and spiritual songs. Sing and make music in your heart to the Lord...'* (Eph. 5:18). The use of instrumental music can greatly help to develop and enhance an inspiring atmosphere of worship and praise in both private and public settings (Ps. 150).

f. One of the first marks of a Spirit-filled life in the early church was that of **speaking in tongues**: *'All of them were filled with the Holy Spirit and began to speak in other tongues as the Spirit enabled them'* (Acts 2:4). This was not only intended as a witness to unbelievers of the works of God (Acts 2:8-11, 1 Cor. 14:22), but was also a God-given means by which believers could edify and strengthen themselves spiritually in their inner life: *'He who speaks in a tongue edifies himself...'* (1 Cor. 14:4). Such edification plays an important part in the growth of the spiritual life of believers and is to be encouraged. Believers can also pray, sing and praise in tongues (1 Cor. 14:14f).

g. On the day of Pentecost, Peter proclaimed that the filling with the Holy Spirit would result in **a whole variety of different charismatic manifestations in believers' lives.** These included God speaking to believers through dreams and visions, and believers prophesying (Acts 2:17). The life of the early church was also characterized by powerful healing miracles and by the release of people from demonic oppression.

Furthermore, Paul encourages believers to eagerly desire other charismatic gifts such as word of wisdom, word of knowledge, faith, gifts of healing, miracles, prophecy, discerning of spirits, speaking in different kinds of tongues, and the interpretation of tongues (1 Cor. 12:7-11 and see 1 Cor. 12:31, 14:1).

h.   When believers learn to live their lives close to God and are consistently filled with the Holy Spirit, they become **sensitive to the inner voice and guidance of the Holy Spirit within their own spirit**: *'The Spirit told Philip...'* (Acts 8:29, 10:19). The believers in all seven churches in Revelation chs. 2-3 were exhorted to *'hear what the Spirit says to the churches'* (Rev. 2:7, etc.). **Learning to live out of our relationship with the Holy Spirit who dwells within us is a crucial lesson**, and so learning to recognize, hear and follow the Holy Spirit as he gives inward promptings, speaks to us, guides us, works and operates through the gifts, and so on, is a major key to growth, expansion and success in ministry.

i.   The Holy Spirit is the One who births **his dynamic vision within believers for the work of God's kingdom.** When Jesus was filled with the Holy Spirit, he was led by the Spirit into the wilderness to overcome Satan and thereafter led into his own ministry (Luke 3:21 – 4:14). Similarly, the early apostles were moved into mission as they obeyed the prompting of the Holy Spirit (see Acts 8:26-29, 10:19-21, 13:1-4, 16:6-10). Believers who learn to hear and follow the Holy Spirit in obedience find themselves being caught up actively in his vision for ministry and mission in the present powerful working of God, as he uses them to work out his purposes in his kingdom and to bring into being new works of God.

It is to fulfil this overarching purpose of God that the Holy Spirit was sent: to raise up a worldwide community of people who are inwardly conscious that Jesus has been exalted to the highest place and that he is Lord over all; who are inwardly conscious that they are the anointed sons and daughters of God (1 John 2:20) who are growing into the maturity of *'the whole measure of the fullness of Christ'* (Eph. 4:13), and who are empowered and led by the Spirit of God to bring about the manifestation, growth and spread of the works of the kingdom of God in this present world.

Ask, seek, knock

God yearns that we be filled with the Holy Spirit in the fullest way possible and that we be open to allow him to move in our lives. He knows far better than we do that experiencing the infilling of the Holy Spirit with all the marks and signs that then accompany this, is so critically important for us in order to live effective lives as believers in witness and ministry, fulfilling the purposes of God for us in this world. Jesus underlined this desire on God's part that we be filled when he said *'how much more will your Father in heaven give the Holy Spirit to those who ask him?'* (Luke 11:13).

Being filled with the Holy Spirit is normally an experience distinct from simply becoming a Christian. Although we are born again through the working of the Holy Spirit within us (John 3:5-8), yet the <u>empowering</u> of our lives is normally an experience distinct from this. Pentecostal and charismatic believers often call the initial experience of being filled with the Holy Spirit after conversion, the 'baptism in the Holy Spirit' (Acts 1:5).

Various phrases are used in the book of Acts to describe when the Holy Spirit initially fills a person. It talks of the Holy Spirit 'coming upon' people (Acts 8:16, 10:44, 19:6), being 'poured out' on people (Acts 2:17, 10:45) and it describes the Holy Spirit 'falling' powerfully on people (Acts 10:44, 11:15 AV). Sometimes this infilling might happen to believers spontaneously (e.g. Acts 10:44-45), or it might happen when church leaders lay their hands on them and pray for this to happen (e.g. Acts 8:15-17, 19:6).

So we need to ask God to fill us with the Holy Spirit and to learn how to be open to the Holy Spirit, so that we can live a consistently Spirit-filled life and see empowerment in ministry. Jesus' promise to us is clear:

'So I say to you: Ask and it will be given to you; seek and you will find; knock and the door will be opened to you. For everyone who asks receives; he who seeks finds; and to him who knocks the door will be opened. Which of you fathers, if your son asks for a fish, will give him a snake instead? Or if he asks for an egg, will give him a scorpion? If you then, though you are evil, know how to give good gifts to your children, how much more will your Father in heaven give the Holy Spirit to those who ask him?' (Luke 11:9-13).

Seek, and may you be filled to overflowing!

6

BASIC SPIRITUAL DISCIPLINES

'My heart says of you, "Seek his face!" Your face, LORD, I will seek' (Ps. 27:8)

'Very early in the morning, while it was still dark, Jesus got up, left the house and went off to a solitary place, where he prayed' (Mark 1:35)

IT should be obvious to anyone who has been a follower of Jesus for any length of time, that growth in our spiritual life does not come automatically.

Although we enter the Christian life through the gateway of repentance and faith, and although it is God's desire for us to live a Spirit-filled life, yet simply being a Spirit-filled Christian in and of itself, does not guarantee that we will keep on growing as we should. Spiritual life does not grow in a vacuum, and we cannot afford to think that we can live our daily lives in highly secularized, busy and often distracted and stressful environments without these asphyxiating our spiritual life or without becoming conditioned to the surrounding secular lifestyle and its own values.

In order to be able to grow in our spiritual life as we should, it is important for us to learn to live and walk as Jesus did, in his <u>total</u> life or, as Willard puts it, we need to live 'as he lived in the entirety of his life – adopting his overall lifestyle.'[3]   When we look at Jesus' life, we can see that he regularly practised what are known as **spiritual disciplines.**   For example, it was his custom to go to the synagogue every Sabbath (Luke 4:16); he fasted for a period of forty days before he began his ministry (Luke 4:1-2); he would often spend time seeking his Father's face in prayer (Mark 1:35; Luke 9:28-29, 22:41-45), and so on.   The practice of these disciplines was the source of the inner peace, strength and spiritual power that he needed to live and minister in the world of his day.

There are several such practices which will help us to grow spiritually, and some basic ones are outlined below.

a.   *Becoming part of a local church family*

The Israelites of the Old Testament were required to keep the Sabbath every week as a holy day (Lev. 23:2-3).   One of the purposes of the Sabbath day was to get the Israelites away from work, and from its distractive busyness and the tiredness it produces, for one full day each week.   This would then enable them to attend the synagogue and to focus on God, prayer and the teachings of his word on this day, to meet with other believers and also to get physically refreshed.   The word of God, prayer and fellowship, therefore, would not be squeezed out of their lives because of incessant work.

---

[3]   Willard, D. *The Spirit of the Disciplines*, London: Hodder and Stoughton, 1996, p.6.

Attendance at the synagogue in this way was Jesus' custom (Luke 4:16), and going to gatherings of believers on the first day of the week similarly became the custom of the early Christians (Acts 2:42, 20:7).

Attending or taking part in meetings and activities which are organized by our church ensures that we are influenced positively and blessed by being with other believers, by the godly atmosphere of worship, prayer and faith, by receiving nourishment from God's word for our spiritual life, and by being edified in the presence of God. Doing this at least twice a week helps us to maintain blessing in our spiritual life during the whole week, and also helps us to develop relationships with other believers.

Furthermore, committing ourselves to a particular group of God's people helps us to get rooted into the life of a local church community, and so helps us to develop the relationships and accountability we need in our personal discipleship and growth as believers. It also helps us in developing close friendships and in meeting our need for social interaction. The subject of becoming rooted into a church family is explored in chapter 7.

b. *Solitude and quietness*

For many people, including believers, life today is often characterized by increasing levels of busyness and stress; by almost endless distractions or spending many hours in legitimate pleasures; by the demands of people or of situations, and by the tyranny of 'what needs to be done.' As a consequence, many believers find it a challenge to manage their time and energy in such a way as to make their relationship with God their first priority in daily life.

59

However, rather than allowing ourselves to simply be the servants of life's daily demands, **we should make proactive use of our time in order to seek first the kingdom of God.** It is the discipline of solitude and quietness which helps us to do this. Seeking a time and place of solitude is perhaps the most basic discipline of all in a believer's individual spiritual life. Learning to regularly 'come away from it all' is crucial to maintaining the freshness of our relationship with God and to ongoing growth in our spiritual life. **It is the key to developing our relationship with the Holy Spirit.**

Distractions and constant busyness cause spiritual life to wane and bring about coldness and distance between ourselves and God in our walk with him. Indeed, Satan is quite happy for us to be running around with busyness even in God's work, if it means that we neglect our personal walk with God. He would seek to steal this from us, if he can, so we need to be proactive in making sure that we keep to this discipline of seeking solitude, rather than passively allowing life to dictate to us how we spend our time. In this regard, sometimes we might need to say 'No' to demands made upon us by others, so that our energies are not so consumed that we have none left for God himself.

Jesus practised this discipline of solitude and quietness in his own life. He rose early in the morning and deliberately sought out a place where he could be alone and quiet, and where he could spend time with God and pray. It was only after this that he began his day's work (Mark 1:35-38). He exhorted his disciples to practise this discipline when he taught them that, in order to be able to pray effectively, they should go *'into your room, close the door and pray to your Father, who is unseen'* (Matt. 6:6).

Having such a quiet place of solitude, helps us to get alone with God and to pray, read his word and commune with him. This is often known as 'having a quiet time.' As we practise this, it then gives God the opportunity he needs to give us the inner peace and strength that arise within us when we dwell and linger in his presence, and this inner strength then helps us to face the challenges of the day.

This 'early morning model' which the life of Jesus gives us is very helpful. If our first challenge is to get away and 'close the door' on the 'outward noise' of busyness and demands, in order to get into a quiet place with God, then the second challenge that we then face is dealing with the 'inward noise' of our thoughts, feelings and stresses caused by daily living.

Being unable to focus in our 'quiet time' is often caused by wandering thoughts and internal stress. Such 'inward noise' is normally greater during the latter part of the day, when we have been through a whole day of work and busyness. So, **having a 'quiet time' is much easier to practise in the earlier hours of the day** when we are fresher after a night's sleep, and are much less distracted and therefore freer within ourselves to focus on prayer and reading the word of God.

c. *Confession*

When we enter into the presence of God in our daily 'quiet time' and attempt to get still before him, often the first thing we become aware of is ourselves and our inward condition. As we seek his holy presence, we may become aware in our conscience of an area of failure in our life, a particular sin which we have committed in thought, word or deed, or a selfish or unkind attitude which we have displayed towards someone else, etc.

When this happens, God in his mercy is making us aware of what we need to confess to him in order to then receive his forgiveness and cleansing in our lives. To enter his holy presence, we must first deal with such things in ourselves, and confession of them to God is the key.

The Bible teaches that *'If we confess our sins, he is faithful and just and will forgive us our sins and purify us from all unrighteousness'* (1 John 1:9). When we have confessed those particular sins and failures which we are consciously aware of and seek his forgiveness, we should then accept, receive and embrace his promise of forgiveness and cleansing. This brings us into a state of inward peace, and enables us to relax in his holy presence and to receive more from him, assured of his mercy and love for us.

d. *Prayer*

Praying expresses our relationship with God. It is, quite simply, talking naturally to him and expressing our heart to him. We often pray when we are alone with God in our 'quiet time' and when we are reading the word of God, although we can pray at any time, of course. Jesus expected his followers to pray: he said, *'when you pray...'* rather than *'if you pray...'* (Matt. 6:5).

Prayer has many forms. We can confess our failures and sins. We can thank him for his faithfulness and goodness to us. We can ask him to fulfil and meet our personal needs or those of people that we know (a form of prayer often known as 'petition'). We can also praise and worship him in song and with music, adoring him and expressing our love for him in this way, as David did in the Psalms. We can pray in tongues or in our own language. It is a good practice to fill our homes with an atmosphere of praise, by using praise CDs whenever we can, as this helps to maintain a spirit of praise in our lives.

Praying together regularly with a group of other believers, either in church meetings or perhaps in a smaller group setting, helps us to grow together in unity and relationship with other believers, and brings about growth in our spiritual life, and it is especially encouraging when we see answers to prayer. There are many examples in Scripture of believers praying together (e.g. Acts 1:14, 2:42, 12:5, 13:2-3). Spending time together regularly in prayer with a close friend can create a deeper level of intimacy and openness in prayer than is possible in a larger group. Becoming a member of a church prayer team or being on a prayer chain, helps us to get more experience in praying for and supporting others in their time of need.

e. *Meditation on the word of God*

Reading the Bible is a source of feeding our spiritual life. When we read it, God speaks to us. The word of God is spiritual food and nourishment to us: God's words are our life (Deut. 32:47), and Jesus said his words are *'spirit and life'* (John 6:63). Just as our bodies need feeding several times every day, so our spiritual life needs feeding regularly from God's word. The apostle Peter said: *'Like newborn babies, crave pure spiritual milk, so that by it you may grow up in your salvation'* (1 Peter 2:2). So we read and study the word of God in order to feed our spiritual life, to strengthen our faith, to understand God's commandments, to know his promises and his wisdom, and to learn his ways.

However, rather than simply reading the word of God just as we would read any other book, it is important that we meditate on it and think deeply about what we read. As we delight ourselves in the word of God and meditate on it, and as we put into practice what we are learning, in obedience to it, then we begin to grow spiritually and bear fruit. As we increasingly learn to walk in God's wisdom and ways, we prosper and are successful in what we do (cf. Josh. 1:8, Ps. 1:1-3). **Our knowledge of the word of God becomes practical and experiential, rather than merely theoretical.** We should learn to meditate on God's promises, to confess them and to stand on them and, as we do this, the word of God enters deeply into our spirits and begins to produce its life-changing effects.

We are normally fed regularly on the word of God in church meetings and small groups, but, in addition to this, it is good to develop the use of other resources to read and study the word. There are many good Christian books available which will help us to grow in our understanding of the word of God and we can also use other resources, such as the internet or Christian television programmes. The Bible is also available for use on mobile devices. Your pastor can help guide you in finding suitable sources for your growth. A good basic guide is to read and meditate on at least one chapter a day from the Bible, and also to do some other devotional reading every day.

f. *Fasting*

Fasting is an important spiritual discipline but which is all too often neglected in church life today. It was regularly practised by believers in the Bible, and Jesus assumed that his followers would also learn to practise this discipline in their lives: he said, '*When you fast...*' rather than '*If you fast...*' (Matt. 6:16). Scripture highlights the importance of fasting by relating several examples of occasions when people fasted either as individuals or together corporately as the people of God.

The practice of fasting is important to the development of our spiritual life and our walk with God, and so the fact that it is not always dealt with in teaching or discipleship at local church level would suggest that we deal with it more fully in a separate chapter (see chapter 10).

g. *Serving*

Servanthood is the heart of Christian work and ministry, and in many ways it exemplifies the opposite of the self-centred values of the world which so often emphasize success, recognition and position. Jesus underlined this when he said: *'...whoever wants to be great among you must be your servant, and whoever wants to be first must be your slave – just as the Son of Man did not come to be served, but to serve...'* (Matt. 20:26-28). His practical example of washing the feet of the disciples would have brought this lesson home to them (John 13:1-17). We serve because he served: *'I have set you an example that you should do as I have done for you... no servant is greater than his master'* (John 13:15-16).

The use of the Greek word *latreia*, variously translated as both 'worship' and 'service' (e.g. Rom. 12:1), shows the connection between the life of worship that we experience as we relate to God, and how this worship of God then works itself out in a life of service in the work of his kingdom. Jesus also underlined this connection: *'Worship the Lord your God, and serve him only'* (Matt. 4:10). To know and follow the Master is also to serve (John 12:26).

True heart worship should lead naturally into a desire to serve. Regular worship without serving leads to a frustration of the purpose of God for us. Serving others is an outworking of our worship of God. To love God means to then also love our neighbour. In our local church, serving can find expression in committing ourselves to becoming active in at least one area of the life of the church (perhaps in the various program activities, in practical work and help, or in the church's outreach and mission activities), and also in serving other people around us in daily life as opportunity or need arises, whether in school/college, the work-place or in the community.

Serving others in such ways can fulfil several purposes. It helps us to see beyond ourselves and to develop vision for the work of God's kingdom. It may also lead to getting involved in a particular ministry that we may desire to take part in. It helps us to put our talents, skills and gifts to use in God's kingdom. It helps us to build relationships with other believers and so creates a closer 'family feeling' in church life. It helps us to fulfil God's call for us to love our neighbour in doing good works, and, serving others brings the blessing of God into our lives: *'Now that you know these things, you will be blessed if you do them'* (John 13:17). In particular, witnessing to non-believers through serving them may well help them to become more open to hearing what we have to say about God. Serving them through deed and life example backs up any words that we speak about the gospel.

h. *Giving*

Giving is an expression of the life of God's kingdom, and is closely connected to serving: Jesus came *'...**to serve, and to give** his* *life as a ransom for many'* (Matt. 20:28). We are to *'give to the one who asks you, and do not turn away from the one who wants to borrow from you'* (Matt. 5:42).

Although we perhaps naturally think in terms of financial giving, we can also give in many other ways, e.g. giving practical help to those in need; giving our time, skills and energy to an aspect of God's work; giving of our wisdom to someone who is seeking it; giving ourselves to a particular outreach ministry; giving by opening our home for hospitality; giving food to needy people through the local foodbank; giving to other charitable causes; even something as simple as giving a smile may bring encouragement to person who is downcast, and so on. Giving freely to others is a mark of God's grace working in us. We give, because God has freely given to us – *'Freely you have received, freely give'* (Matt. 10:8, Eph. 1:6).

The particular aspect of financial giving is discussed later, in chapter 9.

7

ROOTING OURSELVES INTO A CHURCH FAMILY

'...God's household, which is the church of the living God, the pillar and foundation of the truth' (1 Tim. 3:15)

'And we are his household...' (Heb. 3:6)

Church: a family of believers

THE church of Jesus Christ is a worldwide community of redeemed people from *'every nation, tribe, people and language'* (Rev. 7:9). As believers we are all different. We come from different kinds of ethnic and linguistic backgrounds and cultures, we face different kinds of circumstances and may struggle with different issues in life, but, if we are truly born again, we are all people that have experienced the grace, love and salvation that God has given us in Jesus.

The language used in Scripture of relationships among born-again believers is that of family. We call one another 'brother' or 'sister' (Acts 28:14-15, Rom. 16:1); Paul talks of having 'fathers' in the faith (1 Cor. 4:15); the church is described as God's 'household' or family (1 Tim. 3:15, Heb. 3:6), and so on. So as believers we have two families: a natural family into which we were born, and a spiritual family, the worldwide Body of Christ, into which we were born again when we received Jesus into our lives. Furthermore, as people become believers and as their families also get saved and come to church, the church community itself becomes a 'family of families.'

So it is natural that we should want to get to know and relate to our extended spiritual family, certainly in our own geographical area. However, it is also important that we become committed to a local expression of church in particular. Our local church is a community in which we are regularly together with other believers, in which we can therefore come to feel 'at home,' and in which we can put down our spiritual roots, settle and grow together as a family in the faith.

Commitment to family community

Regularly attending a local church and its meetings and program activities, gives us access to taking part in worship and receiving regular teaching from the word of God which will build us up in the faith, as well as enabling us to develop a few 'family friendships' along the way.

However, to fulfil the New Testament aim of growing to maturity in the faith, we need to understand that attendance alone does not go far enough. Growth to maturity through discipleship is not something that happens to us in individual isolation. Many issues in our growth can only be addressed and/or developed in the context of our ongoing commitment to our particular local church family and the relationships that we have in it.[4] **So we need to move on from merely being attendees or from being spectators on the periphery of church life** (keeping ourselves at a 'safe distance' in relationships by maintaining these at a superficial level week by week)**, and become committed participants, rooting ourselves into the life of our church family. If we do not become rooted in church family life, we may remain spiritually immature in many ways.** It says of the early believers that *'they devoted themselves… to the fellowship'* (Acts 2:42).

Learning to love our neighbour

The local church in which we feel 'at home' and into which we decide to root ourselves, is a gift given to us by God. Our participation in this church family helps us to grow in our knowledge of God. Padilla observes that, because the knowledge of God is experienced personally, it is therefore inseparable from our life in church community. Our 'neighbour in church' is growing in his/her knowledge of God, much as we are ourselves, and so we cannot grow to maturity in our own knowledge of God in isolation from our 'neighbour in church.'[5] Participation in the church family gives us the opportunity to learn to fulfil God's two basic commandments, to love him and to love our neighbour (Matt. 22:36-40), and to fulfil the New Testament exhortations to love and care for one another (e.g. 1 John 4:11-12).

---

[4] See Hirsch, A. with Altclass D. *The Forgotten Ways Handbook: A Practical Guide for Developing Missional Churches*, Grand Rapids: Brazos Press, e-Book Edition, 2011.

[5] Padilla, R. "The Contextualization of the Gospel" in *Mission Between the Times*, Grand Rapids: Eerdmans, 1985, p87.

In a sense, the whole of life – whether it is our relationship with God, or our marriage and family relationships, or with our colleagues and friends at work or school, or simply with our neighbour down the street – is about learning how to live in relationship with others.

Life in our church family is no different. As we root ourselves into its life, we can get to know our 'neighbours in church' and learn how to relate wisely to them and to love them, and so fulfil God's commandment, rather than simply worship God together. Sometimes we may even find that some of them are not actually born again yet, or are merely religious.

In the all-round environment of our church's life we can be discipled and grow in our faith. We will be enriched by our interaction with people who may be very different from us. We can learn how to serve, work and have fun together both in and outside of church meetings. We can learn the values of caring for and helping one another practically; of encouraging, standing with and supporting one another in times of need and crisis; of working issues through patiently, wisely and with grace when there are relational tensions, and of practising forgiveness and reconciliation, and so on.

The relaxed openness, relational closeness and trust that participation in a house- or cell-group in particular can create, can help us to develop and practise these holistic values and thereby build more meaningful, loving and trusting relationships. This can then help us in terms of opening ourselves up to others and learning to live together in family community, and it can also help us in terms of being accountable for the way in which we live our lives outside of church meetings. This all-round environment leads into healthy spiritual and relational growth. Furthermore, as we learn to practise these values in the life of our church family, we can also begin to practise some of them in our relationships with non-believing 'neighbours' around us, and this may then perhaps attract them into our church.

It should be obvious that merely attending church once a week on Sunday morning, although this is good and healthy in and of itself, is simply not enough to create the kind of committed relationships and to practise the kind of holistic values which are described above, and inevitably therefore cannot in many ways fulfil God's purpose for us of growing together as disciples of Christ. Establishing these kinds of practical, holistic values requires a commitment to meeting and engaging with other believers at least twice every week as a minimum norm, so both on Sundays and during the week.

Our mutual commitment to relationship with one another in church family community, in and through the nitty-gritty issues of worshipping, serving and socializing together, going through both good times and difficult times together in the heat of real-life issues, produces growth to maturity together in the faith and can result in lifelong friendships developing among believers.

There are many verses in the New Testament epistles which exhort us in regard to our relationships with one another, such as the following:

'Be devoted to **one another** *in brotherly love'* (Rom. 12:10)

'Live in harmony with **one another**' (Rom. 12:16)

*'Accept **one another**, then, just as Christ accepted you...'*
(Rom. 15:7)

*'...rather, serve **one another** in love'* (Gal. 5:13)

*'...be patient, bearing with **one another** in love'* (Eph. 4:2)

*'Be kind and compassionate to **one another**, forgiving each other,...'*
(Eph. 4:32)

*'Submit to **one another** out of reverence for Christ'* (Eph. 5:21)

*'Therefore encourage **one another** and build each other up...'*
(1 Thess. 5:11)

*'Therefore confess your sins to **each other** and pray for **each other** so that you may be healed'* (Jas. 5:16)

*'Finally, all of you, live in harmony with **one another**;...'*
(1 Peter 3:8)

*'And this is his command: to love **one another**...'* (1 John 3:23)

Valuing the family we have been given

The relationships that we have with other believers that God has given us in our church family are far more important than any activity we do in church. **People are a gift to us from God, and so we need to learn to value our church family and the relationships that we have with them.** Of course, this runs counter to the conditioning of secular society in which relationships tend to be utilitarian (i.e. we use people for what we can get, but otherwise stay distant from them) and in which self-centred pleasure- and entertainment-seeking seem to take priority. Knowing that we belong to a community of people that genuinely show commitment and care is an important antidote to the loneliness and social isolation that many people feel today, going a long way to fulfilling our basic human need for social interaction and friendship.

This then suggests the following principles:

a. *Avoid a consumer attitude*

The common consumer attitude of secular culture – sometimes found even amongst believers! – which begins with questions such as: 'What can I get out of this? What can this church give me?' is essentially self-centred thinking which wants to receive without committing to meaningful relationships. However, if we were to begin with questions such as: 'What part can I play? What can I contribute? How can I help in serving together with you?' in addition to also asking 'What can this church give me?', then we are more likely to grow in our discipleship and to develop closer, mutually committed relationships.

b. *Don't criticize your church for its weaknesses*

We should recognize that every church has its own particular strengths and weaknesses, much as any family does. Our own church is no exception. We should learn to recognize and value its strengths, and to pray and commit ourselves to helping our leaders to find ways in which its weaknesses may be effectively addressed. **Leaders are not perfect, they cannot do everything and they need our support, not our criticism.** Despite a church's imperfections, if we spend long enough in it, we will doubtless find marks of God's grace and love there. If 'the grass appears to be greener' in another church, then we must learn not to criticize our own church. It is also true that, if we spend long enough in that other church, then we will become aware of its own weaknesses, not just its strengths. Don't forget that **every believing community of God's people is a work of grace in progress**, just as we ourselves are!

c. *Don't drift from church to church*

Some believers make the mistake of effectively becoming rootless drifters, spending some time in one church and then leaving it for another church, and so on. Such rootless drifting, perhaps seeking to find that 'something special' or going where the 'grass appears to be greener' for a while, hinders that person's discipleship and growth to spiritual maturity. It leaves him/her without committed relationships and the support and accountability that come through these. Having significantly fewer meaningful and committed relationships then leaves the person more isolated and therefore also more spiritually vulnerable. If the person is unable for whatever reason to relate effectively to other people, such wandering can also become a way of running away from dealing with issues in his/her personal life. What became an undealt-with issue in one church, often then becomes an issue again in the next church they attend. Such rootless drifters tend not to want to be submissive towards spiritual leadership, and so they wander instead of learning to stay and get rooted, growing and serving together with others in a healthy way.

d. *Don't walk off, work things through*

As in a natural family, in church there can sometimes be tensions in relationships, or things can go wrong. This is where we need to learn to apologize, to work things through, and to forgive hurts etc., as much as it lies within us. We cannot afford to simply walk off without dealing with things properly. Rather, we should see problems and issues as opportunities to help us to grow and mature together. **The message of Christianity is that relationships are redeemable.** We are reconciled to God (2 Cor. 5:20), so we should learn to forgive and to be reconciled with each other as well. **This biblical value contrasts with the tendency in secular culture today in which breaking and abandoning relationships, with the resulting inward brokenness and heart wounds, has sadly become all too common.**

Walking off elsewhere without resolving our problem and speaking badly about those we have left, or, conversely, staying and not dealing with it, which can lead to bitterness in our hearts and gossip, are both wrong scenarios. Forgiveness and reconciliation ought to be the aim: *'Love covers over a multitude of sins'* (1 Peter 4:8). If we feel we must leave, then at least we ought to work things through, forgive and then leave in peace.

Walking off and abandoning relationships not only hurts those we leave behind (including leaders and children in the church) – hurts which can then take several months to heal – it also shows how little value we attach to the relationships God has given us. **It is a denial of learning to love our neighbour.** It can also leave our children hurt, which can then potentially become a seed of bitterness in their hearts towards church as they grow up.

Some good fruits of being rooted

Rooting ourselves into the life of a church family:

a. gives us an accepting environment in which we have the opportunity to practise life-applied lessons we are learning about discipleship and following Jesus, and it helps us to become accountable about how we are living our lives, as we are discipled;

b. helps us to receive healing for past relational hurts and to learn how to develop healthy relationships, working issues through properly together, rather than continuing in any dysfunctional relational patterns we may have experienced before we became believers;

c. helps us to get inner life issues dealt with, and so get released and healed, and to deal with any wrong attitudes we may have from time to time, and so mature socially;

d. helps us to learn how to work with our leaders, and to serve together with other believers;

e. makes us **a friendly, attractive community** which other people may want to join and which demonstrates the truth of the gospel in life: *'By this all men will know that you are my disciples, if you love one another'* (John 13:35).

Relating to our church leaders

As we root ourselves into our local church, we need to learn to see the role of our leaders from God's perspective. They are appointed to minister to, to care for and to teach and disciple us in the faith, and this is a work and responsibility for which they will be required to give an account (Heb. 13:17). Although all leaders are themselves growing in the faith, and certainly have weaknesses and occasional failings, yet we ought to maintain a healthy attitude towards their position and work: they are appointed to their task and given their mandate by God himself.

The main aim for which leaders in the body of Christ are called, is to minister into our lives so that we grow to maturity in the faith and ourselves become ready to minister to others, according to the particular calling and gifts that we have been given by the Lord. This is outlined by Paul in Ephesians 4:12-14, as below:

'...to prepare God's people for works of service, so that the body of Christ may be built up until we all reach unity in the faith and in the knowledge of the Son of God and become mature, attaining to the whole measure of the fullness of Christ. Then we will no longer be infants...' (Eph. 4:12-14)

The Greek word *katartismos* used in verse 12, variously translated as 'to prepare' or 'perfecting,' has the meaning of bringing a work to completion, and the word *eis* translated as 'for' actually means 'into.' So the words in verse 12 could be rendered in a simple way like this: 'to get God's people ready to be in the work of ministry.' Hence, it is not God's purpose that we remain simply adherents in our local church, being ministered to or taking part in activities regularly. **The purpose of God is that we ourselves become ready to serve the Lord in whatever ministry the Lord directs us into.**

So a primary responsibility of church leaders is to do what they can to be a part of this process of raising us up as God's people and preparing us to minister ourselves. Much of this preparation at local church level consists of pastoral care, teaching and discipleship, as well as giving us experience and mentoring us in carrying some kind of responsibility in the various activities and programs of the church. These should not be looked upon as an end in themselves, but as part of a wider purpose of God for us in which he is attempting to prepare us for some kind of ministry.

We should, therefore, avoid developing any critical or cynical attitudes towards our leaders. Such attitudes do not build up a positive and fruitful relationship between believers and leaders. Indeed, critical attitudes are effectively doing Satan's work for him; they simply undermine the potential of this relationship and make it harder for leaders to undertake the responsibilities of their work with joy and success. **We should honour leaders and submit to their leadership,** so that healthy growth in the faith can come about in our lives. When we are not submissive, or when we criticize or gossip about leaders behind their backs, or when we stop listening to them or receiving from their ministry, then it is our own growth that is hindered. This is not to our advantage, according to Hebrews 13:17.

'Obey your leaders and submit to their authority. They keep watch over you as men who must give an account. Obey them so that their work will be a joy, not a burden, for that would be of no advantage to you' (Heb. 13:17)

When we see that God's purpose is that we gain from our leaders, that we grow under their ministry and eventually begin to take part in ministry ourselves, then we have understood what the advantage is for us in submitting to them. It is to our advantage that we submit to them, that we support their vision, and that we pray for them and for the work that they do. For example, Jonathan Edwards emphasized the need for us to pray for our leaders, rather than succumbing to a negative, complaining attitude:

'If some Christians that have been complaining of their ministers had said and acted less before men and had applied themselves with all their might to pray to God for their ministers – had, as it were, risen and stormed heaven with their humble, fervent and incessant prayers for them – they would have been much more in the way of success.'[6]

So, an essential part of the work of leaders is to try to make sure that we as believers are growing in our faith in a healthy and consistent way. The process of discipleship, of growth in the knowledge of God and his word and ways, and of growth into some kind of ministry activity, necessarily involves **the development of spiritual character and the transformation of attitudes on our part**, including the inevitable need for correction from time to time.

Ministers are seen in Scripture very much as spiritual parents, both as fathers and mothers (see 1 Cor. 4:15; 1 Thess. 2:7,11), and so the relationship between leaders and believers will, in some measure, reflect the parent-child relationship. As part of discipleship, therefore, leaders will need to take believers aside from time to time and correct them, much as any responsible parent has to. Church leaders are not perfect, any more than our parents are perfect. However, it is their responsibility to correct us when needed, just as it is our parents' responsibility.

So as believers we should take a proactive approach to correction, with a view to what positives we can gain from it, rather than simply responding with a reactive, defensive or resistant stance. Correction is essential for all of us from time to time, and challenges

---

[6] Jonathan Edwards, quoted in *Power Through Prayer* by E.M. Bounds, Springdale, USA: Whitaker House, 1982, p.89.

us on points that we need to address in our lives. As a simple example from daily life, part of the challenge to Christian discipleship is to maintain the integrity of the way in which we live our lives and conduct our relationships as believers with other people outside church. In the Book of Proverbs, the willingness to receive correction is valued as wisdom, whereas resisting correction is seen as foolishness (Prov. 10:17; 15:10,12). As we learn to receive and embrace correction, we continue to grow into the Lord's purpose for our lives.

When leaders are attempting to deal with an issue in a person's life which involves a measure of correction, it is important for onlookers (who may be aware that something is going on) to support, pray for and back up the leaders. Not doing this, and perhaps making the mistake of going against the leaders and supporting the person who needs to be corrected, is not only immature, it also makes the job of the leaders more difficult and stressful. Sometimes a source of sin and conflict in church life can be a person who is not willing to submit to leadership or discipleship, or who perhaps is not even born again yet.

8

KEEPING A TIGHT REIN ON OUR TONGUE

'The tongue has the power of life and death, and those who love it will eat its fruit' (Prov. 18:21)

'Do not let any unwholesome talk come out of your mouths, but only what is helpful for building others up according to their needs, that it may benefit those who listen' (Eph. 4:29)

Life and death are in the power of the tongue

THE Bible has much to say about the tongue and how we use it. The tongue has the power to produce both life and death (Prov. 18:21), so we can destroy others (Prov. 11:9) or build them up by the words we speak (Eph. 4:29); or, we can both praise God and curse people with it (Jas. 3:9-10), and so on.

The world of the media, particularly the so-called 'gutter press,' seems to thrive on people's sinful love of gossip, innuendo and scandal, and it feeds us a never-ending diet of information about the personal lives of others (particularly so-called celebrities), much of it of an intimate, sinful, gossipy, often intrusive and sometimes slanderous or libellous nature: *'For out of the overflow of the heart the mouth speaks'* (Matt. 12:34). People whose lives are subjected mercilessly to public scrutiny in this way are only too often left hurt or devastated. James makes strong summary statements on the power of the tongue: *'it is a restless evil, full of deadly poison'* and *'it corrupts the whole person'* (Jas. 3:6,8).

Gossip destroys trust between people

The destructive nature of gossip is noted several times in the book of Proverbs. **In a word, gossip destroys relationships and trust between people.** Let's take perhaps the simplest scenario to illustrate this, with persons A, B and C who know each other. Person A gossips to person B about person C. Person B enjoys hearing about other people, so s/he drinks in what s/he hears: *'The words of a gossip are like choice morsels; they go down to a man's inmost parts'* (Prov. 18:8, 26:22). Person B is foolish, or perhaps simply naïve enough to receive undiscerningly what s/he hears, because *'A simple man believes anything'* (Prov. 14:15). S/he does not think to judge or find out whether what person A is saying is true or false; whether it is the full truth or only partial truth; whether there is another side to the story which needs to be known (Prov. 18:17); whether person A harbours ill-feeling towards person C, especially if what was said was slanderous, character-destroying or without foundation; or, whether it is uncovering something true about person C which would deeply hurt person C if it were made known, and so on.

Having drunk in person A's words, person B now begins to think differently about person C; his/her attitude towards person C is influenced negatively by person A. Person B may also go out and spread it around to yet others, and so the chain of gossip begun by person A continues on, perhaps even developing to become a malicious rumour about person C. One word becomes ten! Person B does not yet understand that *'whoever repeats the matter separates close friends'* (Prov. 17:9) and that *'whoever spreads slander is a fool'* (Prov. 10:18).

The next time person C meets person B, perhaps not yet knowing what has been said behind his/her back, person C notices that person B is responding in a different way towards him/her than normal and remains a little distanced and perhaps even cold. Whether or not it was intentional, the net effect of the gossip is that person A has succeeded in separating persons B and C in their friendship: *'A perverse man stirs up dissension, and a gossip separates close friends'* (Prov. 16:28). When person C finally finds out what has been said about him/her, s/he is very hurt and any trust in his/her relationship with both persons A and B breaks down. Person B then feels like a fool for believing what was said and for perhaps spreading it around, and begins to distance him/herself from person A. So the relationships between each of the three people are damaged.

The word of God has many references to the evil of gossip and its sister sins, slander and mockery. It is interesting that one of the Greek words used for slander is *diaballo*, which is related to the word *diabolos* which means 'devil.' Slander (that is, speaking about someone in such a way as to defame their character in the minds of others) truly is the devil's work! We are warned about the dangers of *'slinking about as a talebearer'* (Lev. 19:16), and about spreading false reports, giving false testimony, being a malicious witness, and speaking against our brothers (Ex. 20:16, 23:1; Jas. 4:11). In Leviticus 19:16, the word used for 'talebearer' refers to a person who goes about as a scandal-monger. Proverbs 6:16-19 gives us a list of seven things which the LORD hates, and among them are the following: a lying tongue, a false witness who pours out lies, and a man who stirs up dissension among brothers.

Gossip (and particularly slander) destroys trust between people, separating friends. **It can also cause mistrust to develop between believers and church leaders.** Its root cause may be simply a loose, uncontrolled tongue, or, sometimes, it can have a root of self-interest at its heart. The old cliché that idle hands do the devil's work is affirmed by Paul: idleness can lead to gossiping and becoming busybodies, with such people going around *'saying things they ought not to'* (1 Tim. 5:13). The fruit of gossip may be suspicion, false rumours, fear, the formation of cliques, lying, the breaking of friendships, unforgiveness and bitterness, and so on. If not dealt with, it can undermine and destroy a pastor's work and even the whole life of a church community: *'consider what a great forest is set on fire by a small spark'* (Jas. 3:5). **In a word, gossip is destructive, poisonous and evil.**

Gossip amongst believers outside church meetings (e.g. 1 Tim. 5:13), or among family members at home about other people in church, about the leaders of the church and/or problems in the life of the church, is problematic for the ongoing spiritual life of a church community. Sometimes believers can quite literally talk themselves out of the blessing they received at church, and then they wonder why their spiritual lives are not consistently blessed! Such inappropriate or negative talk, particularly in the presence of children or unsaved family members, tends to have a negative effect on all concerned. **Believers, and particularly children or unsaved family members, may become embittered, thinking that church**

is just a hive of relational problems, and it comes as no surprise then if children in particular grow up and develop a negative attitude towards church life, perhaps even ending up not wanting to go to church at all. **The seeds of such bitterness were sown in their own homes by believing family members through inappropriate conversations about other people.**

We would do well to heed the words of James: *'If anyone considers himself religious and yet does not keep a tight rein on his tongue, he deceives himself and his religion is worthless'* (Jas. 1:26). In the words of the well-known poster, often used during the Second World War: 'Careless talk costs spiritual lives!'

Building confidence and trust in church life

In order to fulfil the mandate of loving God and loving our neighbour in church life, **we need to aim to create an atmosphere of trust and confidence amongst ourselves as a family of believers.** Developing such a climate can then lead on to being more open with one another, accepting one another, sharing personal issues with people whom we have learned to trust, working together joyfully, and so on, building relationships between us which have strong foundations.

The key to this is keeping our relationships holy. If I tolerate gossip within my friendship with another person, then this means that I am tolerating within that friendship something which is sinful and which has the power to destroy, and therefore the friendship becomes unholy, both for myself and for my friend. This then not only hinders healthy mutual spiritual growth and blessing within that friendship, it also drags us both down under the negative effects of our gossip, and it will also inevitably and ultimately cause hurt either to myself, my friend, or to others who become victims of our gossip. **To keep a relationship holy, I need to determine that I will not tolerate gossip within it.** In church life, keeping our relationships holy then **helps us to proactively build up the house of God**, refusing to engage in anything like gossip which would undermine its growth and pull it down: *'The wise woman builds her house, but with her own hands the foolish one tears hers down'* (Prov. 14:14). Gossip destroys trust and confidence, making it difficult to fulfil the mandate of creating loving relationships. So driving out gossip is important and, if necessary, so also is disciplining a person who is gossiping: *'Drive out the mocker, and out goes strife; quarrels and insults are ended'* (Prov. 22:10).

Integrity, discretion and wisdom

The many statements in Proverbs about the use of the tongue and its fruit, suggest that **learning NOT to gossip is a matter of gaining wisdom with experience**, going from not understanding the potential damage which can be caused by a loose or foolish tongue, to understanding this, and then to determining to behave in such a way as not to allow such damage to occur. More than this, if the fear of the LORD is the beginning of wisdom (Prov. 1:7) and if we are to be held to account for every idle word we utter (Matt. 12:36), then surely we must learn the wisdom of avoiding gossip. In order to develop mutual trust, believers need to learn to speak with integrity, discretion and wisdom.

a. *Build a good reputation for yourself*

A good reputation is built up over time by developing a godly character, demonstrated through wisdom both learnt and applied. Having a good reputation causes people to trust you. Similarly, but in contrast, a bad reputation is not easily changed. Betraying a confidence through gossip, for instance, will give you the stain of a bad reputation which will be difficult to lose (Prov. 25:9, 29:10). So learn to walk with the wise. Observe and get to know them, understand and imitate their ways, and so become wise yourself (Prov. 13:20). Do what they do, and stay away from people who gossip (Prov. 14:17, 20:19).

b. *Act and speak with integrity*

Learning to communicate with integrity is basic to Christian character development, especially for leaders, and again is basic to developing trust. Integrity can be defined as adherence to moral principles, and as the quality of being honest, sound and unimpaired. Psalm 15:2-3 gives examples of integrity such as speaking the truth from our heart, having no slander on our tongue, and not casting a slur on our fellowman. It is such people who can develop intimacy with the Lord (Ps. 15:1) and walk closely with him. Those who love life and wish to see long days must keep their tongue from evil (Ps. 34:11-13, 1 Peter 3:10). Integrity does not betray a confidence (Prov. 25:9). We are expected to put off slander and lying (Mark 7:22, Col. 3:8, Jas. 4:11). Timothy was exhorted to set an example to other believers in his speech (1 Tim. 4:12). The wives of church leaders, and older women in the church, are expected not to be slanderers (1 Tim. 3:11, Titus 2:3). Keeping our word is a key to developing trust in relationships, so we need to learn to say what we mean, and to mean what we say.

c. *Speak with discretion*

Another key to developing trust is learning discretion (that is, behaving tactfully so as to avoid social embarrassment or distress, especially when it comes to keeping confidences). A discreet person can be trusted to keep a secret (Prov. 11:13), and has learned that covering over an offence quietly is wiser than blurting things out to other people (Prov. 12:23, 17:9, 19:11). In fact, covering over an offence promotes love (Prov. 17:9), rather than creating potential embarrassment. A beautiful woman without discretion can be likened to a gold ring in a pig's snout (Prov. 11:22). Discretion is linked closely to the development of wisdom (Prov. 1:4, 2:11, 5:2). A basic rule of thumb in discretion is to ask yourself whether a particular person actually <u>needs</u> to know what you know about an issue. If not, you shouldn't tell them.

d. *The wisdom of holding your tongue*

Learning to hold our tongue is a lesson we all have to learn in life, and many conflicts and offences are thus avoided: *'When words are many, sin is not absent, but he who holds his tongue is wise'* (Prov. 10:19). Discreet people have learned to hold their tongues and to let matters die down (Prov. 19:11). Where there is no tale-bearer the strife ceases: *'Without wood a fire goes out; without gossip a quarrel dies down'* (Prov. 26:20).

e. *Avoid initiating or getting involved in gossip*

A simple truth regarding gossip is that *'Where words are many, sin is not absent...'* (Prov. 10:19), so we need to learn to avoid idle chatter about other people (1 Tim. 5:13), especially in our own home. Another important rule of thumb is that **if you share personal issues**

with people who gossip, then one day they will also gossip about you, so sooner or later you are bound to get hurt: '*A gossip betrays a confidence; so avoid a man who talks too much*' (Prov. 20:19). In short, learn to mind your own business, and, stay out of things and you won't get hurt. It is a much more positive thing to pray for people, to talk to God about them, than to gossip to others about them.

f. *Determine to build people up in what you say about them to others*

The apostle Paul exhorts us to control our mouths and to speak to or about other people in such a way that it builds them up, rather than pulls them down, so that the fruit of what we say is positive (Eph. 4:29, Isa. 50:4). Some good rules of thumb would be:

- note what is good in a person and gossip about that;

- or, if you really do feel you need to say something negative about a person, then find at least two positive things to say about them as well, to balance out the picture you present of them;

- or, tell other people nothing but what you have already spoken to the person him/herself. Do this in strict confidence, and even then do it only if it really is necessary.

Some other wise sayings relating to gossip

'Wise men store up knowledge, but the mouth of a fool invites ruin' (Prov. 10:14)

'The lips of the righteous know what is fitting, but the mouth of the wicked only what is perverse' (Prov. 10:32)

'A man who lacks judgement derides his neighbour, but a man of understanding holds his tongue' (Prov. 11:2)

'The tongue of the wise commends knowledge, but the mouth of the fool gushes folly' (Prov. 15:2)

'The tongue that brings healing is a tree of life, but a deceitful tongue crushes the spirit' (Prov. 15:4)

'The heart of the righteous weighs its answers, but the mouth of the wicked gushes evil' (Prov. 15:28)

'A wicked man listens to evil lips; a liar pays attention to a malicious tongue' (Prov. 17:4)

'A fool's lips bring him strife, and his mouth invites a beating' (Prov. 18:6)

'A fool's mouth is his undoing, and his lips are a snare to his soul' (Prov. 18:7)

Other helpful rules of thumb

Before sharing something with another person, first ask yourself five questions:

- Are you certain that what you have heard is completely true, or gives the full picture?

  If you are not sure, then find out first whether it is true or not, and then go on to the next four questions.

- Is what you have heard confidential? Can it or should it be shared openly?

  If it is confidential, then keep your mouth shut and don't share it with anyone else. If it can be shared, then still be careful with whom you share it.

- Is it helpful to others to know this thing?

  If it is not helpful to them to know, then simply do not tell them.

- Is it necessary for anyone else to know about it?

  If it is not necessary, then again do not tell anyone else. Tell only people who do actually need to know.

- Do you know the person well with whom you think you may share this information? Does s/he have integrity? Is s/he discreet?

  If you are not sure, then either simply don't tell them anyway, or test them first by telling them something else that is relatively unimportant, and see what they do with it. If they gossip this around, then do not trust this person with the information you are privy to. S/he that is untrustworthy with little, will also be untrustworthy with much (cf. Luke 16:10).

Other useful principles

- If you have anything to say about a person, **then say it to that person**, rather than to other people. If you do not have the courage to do this, then don't say anything at all about him/her to others. If you do say it to him/her, then there is no need at all for you to then relate to others what you have said, as this can still become gossip or the sharing of negative feelings which can perhaps wrongly influence the people you talk to.

- Similarly, **don't gossip about a church leader behind his/her back.** If you have anything to say, then say it to him/her face to face. Don't accept to listen to gossip from other people about a church leader, tell them to go and tell it to that leader face to face, or, if possible, call that leader into the conversation and let them say it to you while the leader is present: *'Do not entertain an accusation against an elder unless it is brought by two or three witnesses'* (1 Tim. 5:19).

- Think about what you intend to say, before you say it (cf. Eph. 4:29), and try to make sure that what you say is appropriate.

- **Learn to become a listener**, rather than a gossiper: *'Let every man be quick to listen, slow to speak...'* (Jas. 1:19).

- If you realize you have a problem with gossiping, then it may help you to make an agreement with your spouse to let him/her hold you accountable regarding what you say about other people. Furthermore, agreeing to 'fast from gossip' for a set number of days in your own home, with the purpose of not saying anything at all about other people in that time period, will help you to catch and stop yourself, as you become aware that you are beginning to do it. It is a profitable exercise to spend quality time **praying for other people, rather than gossiping about them.**

9

FINANCIAL GIVING

'God loves a cheerful giver' (2 Cor. 9:8)

'On the first day of every week, each one of you should set aside a sum of money in keeping with his income...' (1 Cor. 16:2)

THE word of God has a lot to say about our attitude towards and our use of money and material goods. As I said in chapter 6, giving is an expression of the life of God's kingdom. It is intrinsic to our relationship with God and is a regular and weekly part of our worship. Paul described the gift which the church at Philippi sent to him as *'a fragrant offering, an acceptable sacrifice, pleasing to God'* (Phil. 4:18). So when we give to God and his work, we are expressing our desire to serve and honour him.

It is important for us to grow in our understanding of how to manage the money that God has blessed us with. God's work, including the work of our own local church, cannot go forward without money, and our own lives cannot grow, prosper and develop without the blessing of having money. It is also important to realise that the Bible teaches some principles with regards to money and giving which **are different to those which tend to characterize the world of unbelievers**. As we live our daily lives in a secularized environment and become used to the economic principles by which it operates, **it is important to learn also to live by biblical principles as it is these which reap the blessing of God in our lives.** Some of these biblical principles are discussed below.

a. *Stewardship*

The Bible encourages us **to manage our finances properly and to be wise and faithful stewards** of what we have been given (see the parable of the talents recorded in Matt. 25:14-30). Some basic principles of stewardship would include the following. Accountability is an important principle in the kingdom of God (Matt. 24:45-51, 25:14-30; Luke 19:11-26). Good stewardship is rewarded with increase and blessing, whereas bad stewardship leads to loss (Matt. 25:28-29). Squandering wealth leads to poverty (Luke 15:13-16). Living continually in debt is not the will of God (Prov. 22:7, Rom. 13:8). In order to grow, money needs to be invested (Matt. 25:27).

A materialistic attitude towards money does not reflect the wisdom of God. We should not let the love of money control the way we live our lives; it is a root of many evils and can lead us away from God (1 Tim. 6:10). We cannot serve both God and money (Matt. 6:24).

b. *Grace and generosity in giving*
Reading: 2 Corinthians chs. 8-9

The development of grace in regard to giving is emphasized in the New Testament (see 2 Cor. 8:1,6-7,9; 9:8). We should learn to live out of God's grace in every area of our lives, **and doing so in** the area of giving is not an exception: *'See that you also excel in this grace of giving'* (2 Cor. 8:7). The grace which characterized the believers in the Macedonian churches caused them to be generous in their giving towards Paul's appeal to help the churches in Judea, even when they themselves were in need (2 Cor. 8:1-4).

As believers, **we are not immune to fear, worry, stinginess and self-centredness when it comes to money, and learning to express grace in giving helps us to overcome such things and frees us from their grip.** Rather than allowing ourselves to be controlled by such things, we need to develop an understanding and an attitude of faith that embrace God's promises to supply all our needs, and which help us to become free in our giving to others:

'But seek first [God's] kingdom and his righteousness, and all these things will be given to you as well' (Matt. 6:33)

'My God will supply all your needs through his glorious riches in Christ Jesus' (Phil. 4:19)

Generosity with our material goods and our money is the expression of God's grace working in us (2 Cor. 8:2; 9:11,14). The reason why *'God loves a cheerful giver'* (2 Cor. 9:7) is because **free, cheerful generosity reflects his own nature**: he is a gracious, good and generous God. The Greek word *hilaros* used in 2 Corinthians 9:7 means to be 'prompt' or 'willing,' or to be 'merry' or 'cheerful,' and gives us the modern English word 'hilarious.' So when we give freely and cheerfully from our hearts, rather than giving because we feel pressured or manipulated to do so, this reflects his nature and we are learning to become the kind of giver that he is himself.

The deep grace evident in the early community of believers after Pentecost, caused their hearts to open up in sacrificial, free generosity towards those in need, sharing their possessions with one another. Some of them even went as far as to sell land, fields or [second] homes to meet the needs of other believers, so that no-one lacked the basic necessities of daily living:

> *'All the believers were one in heart and mind. No one claimed that any of his possessions was his own, but they shared everything they had... much grace was upon them all. There were no needy persons among them. For from time to time those who owned lands or houses sold them, brought the money from the sales, and put it at the apostles' feet, and it was distributed to anyone as he had need. Joseph... sold a field he owned and brought the money and put it at the apostles' feet'* (Acts 4:32-37)

Such willingness to demonstrate grace, and to be generous in giving to others who are in need, results in closer unity among believers and in heart-felt thanks to God on the part of those who have received:

> *'All the believers were one in heart and mind...'* (Acts 4:32)

> *'...many thanks to God... men will praise God for the obedience that accompanies your confession of the gospel of Christ, and for your generosity in sharing with them... And in their prayers for you their hearts will go out to you, because of the surpassing grace God has given to you'* (2 Cor. 9:12-14)

Furthermore, the willingness to share freely with those who are called to do the work of ministry helps us to partake in the work that they are doing. We become partners with them in the work of the gospel, howbeit in a different form that they themselves are called to.

For example, the church at Philippi gave regularly to Paul towards his needs and his work for the gospel, and sent their gifts to him by the hand of Epaphroditus (Phil 2:25, 4:15-19).

c. *God blesses those who give*

An attitude of generosity causes believers not only to enjoy the spiritual blessing involved in giving, but also to prosper. It is interesting that the Bible teaches that a generous person may think s/he runs the risk of ending up with less, but can actually end up gaining more in the long term, while a stingy person may think s/he is saving, when actually s/he can end up with less in the long term. **God gives to those who give**. We cannot out-give God; he is no-one's debtor.

> *'Good will come to him who is generous and lends freely... he has scattered abroad his gifts to the poor...'* (Ps. 112:5,9)

> *'One man gives freely, yet gains even more; another withholds unduly, but comes to poverty. A generous man will prosper; he who refreshes others will himself be refreshed'* (Prov. 11:24-25)

> *'A generous man will himself be blessed, for he shares his food with the poor'* (Prov. 22:9)

> *'He who gives to the poor will lack nothing...'* (Prov. 28:27)

> *'Give, and it will be given to you. A good measure, pressed down, shaken together and running over, will be poured into your lap. For with the measure you use, it will be measured to you'* (Luke 6:38)

This teaching about freely expressing grace in generous giving, and the blessing of God upon our life which results from it, is associated with the principle of **sowing and reaping**: *'Remember this: Whoever sows sparingly will also reap sparingly, and whoever sows generously will also reap generously'* (2 Cor. 9:6). So, in a word, **if we want to reap much blessing, we need to learn to be willing to sow much.** A farmer who sows only a little seed can expect to reap only a meagre harvest, whereas a farmer who sows much will reap far more than the other. This is a self-evident law of nature. So we should learn to sow in accordance with our expectation to reap, and **we reap because it is in God's own nature to bless:**

> *'Now he who supplies seed to the sower and bread for food will also supply and increase your store of seed and will enlarge the harvest of your righteousness. You will be made rich in every way so that you can be generous on every occasion, and through us your generosity will result in thanksgiving to God'* (2 Cor. 9:10-11)

d. *Tithing*

There are several concepts in the Old Testament to describe the way the Israelites were to give to God, such as offerings, gifts and sacrifices. Another key concept of giving in the Old Testament was that of **tithing** (see Deut. 14:22-29), giving a tenth of one's produce and increase to God. Both Abraham (Gen. 14:20) and Jacob (Gen. 28:22) practised tithing, and it played a key role in the religious life of Israel by supporting the priests' livelihood (Num. 18:21,24,31). Jesus encouraged the Jews of his own day to practise it (Matt. 23:23).

The key principle in tithing was that people would **honour God with the firstfruits of their produce** (see Mal. 3:6-12). They were to honour God by recognizing him as the ultimate source of all their increase and wealth, and to do this **by making him the first priority when planning how to use their income.**

It is important to note that God stressed that **the tithe belonged to him** and not to the people; it was holy to the Lord (Lev. 27:30,32). **Not giving tithes and offerings was tantamount to robbing God of what belonged to him** (Mal. 3:9-10). In Malachi's day, the people had stopped giving their tithes, and God told them that the consequence was that they had come under a curse as a nation, and this curse was affecting the healthy growth of their crops (Mal. 3:9,11). **God specifically told the Israelites to test him in this area of tithing.** He gave them a great promise that if they would return to the practice of tithing, then he would bless them in such great measure that even the surrounding nations would notice it:

> *'Test me in this and see if I will not open the floodgates of heaven and pour out so much blessing that you will not have room enough for it. I will prevent pests from devouring your crops, and the vines in your fields will not cast their fruit... Then all the nations will call you blessed...'* (Mal. 3:10-11)

Although tithing is not specifically enjoined upon believers in the New Testament epistles, yet Paul, as we have seen above, does teach the principle of the growth of inward grace in the area of giving. Tithing, if done from a willing heart, would certainly be an expression of such grace in a believer's life today. Because giving as a Christian is a matter of grace, tithing should not be practised as a matter of religious legalism.

There are many believers today (including myself) who, as they grow in the grace and knowledge of God, have felt the inward compulsion of the Holy Spirit to begin to regularly tithe their income into their local church, and have seen God answer them by not only meeting all their needs, but also by giving them increase. **As they have taken this step of faith and given more, God has given even more back to them.** They have come to understand that God's blessing will be on the 90% of our income, if we first give him the 10% which he says belongs to him.

The practise of tithing has several benefits:

i. it helps believers to plan what they do with their income by putting God first, rather than themselves.

ii. they can then prioritize the work of God's kingdom in their giving.

iii. it releases believers from the inward grip of fear, worry and stinginess.

iv. it frees them up to be able to give abundantly by grace.

v. it allows God to respond to their giving, by blessing them in return.

So *how* should we give?

a. We should give to God and to the work of the ministry.

'Do not store up for yourselves treasures on earth, where moth and rust destroy, and where thieves break in and steal. But store

up for yourselves treasures in heaven, where moth and rust do not destroy and where thieves do not break in and steal. For where your treasure is, there your heart will be also'
(Matt. 6:19-21)

'I have received full payment and even more; I am amply supplied, now that I have received from Epaphroditus the gifts you sent' (Phil. 4:18)

b. We should give what we have freely decided ourselves in our hearts to give. We should not give reluctantly, neither out of a sense of compulsion nor because we feel pressurized to give.

'Each man should give what he has decided in his heart to give, not reluctantly or under compulsion, for God loves a cheerful giver' (2 Cor. 9:7)

c. We should aim to excel in the grace of giving, and therefore give in proportion to our spiritual growth.

'But just as you excel in everything... see that you also excel in this grace of giving' (2 Cor. 8:7)

d. We should plan our giving. We should give regularly, thoughtfully and in keeping with our income, rather than simply giving a few coins or notes taken from our pocket or wallet.

'On the first day of every week, each of you should set aside a sum of money in keeping with his income, saving it up...'
(1 Cor. 16:2)

e. We should give freely, generously and even sacrificially, with enthusiasm and joy.

> *'...they gave as much as they were able, and even beyond their ability'* (2 Cor. 8:3)

> *'Entirely on their own, they urgently pleaded with us for the privilege of sharing in this service to the saints'* (2 Cor. 8:3)

> *'Out of the most severe trial, their overflowing joy and their extreme poverty welled up in rich generosity'* (2 Cor. 8:2)

> *'God loves a cheerful giver'* (2 Cor. 9:7)

10

ON FASTING

'When you fast...' (Matt. 6:16)

'...and your Father, who sees what is done in secret, will reward you' (Matt. 6:18)

THE subject of fasting was touched upon briefly in chapter 6, but, because it is an important spiritual discipline that is all too often neglected in church life, it deserves and needs a chapter all to itself. Fasting is a subject that is not always dealt with in teaching or discipleship at the local church level, and many believers, particularly in the West, either do not practise it at all or do so only rarely, and so fail to appreciate it for the powerful spiritual tool that it is when used regularly. Jonathan Edwards affirmed this when he said:

> 'One thing more I would mention concerning fasting and prayer, wherein I think there has been a neglect in ministers; and that is that although they recommend and much insist on the duty of secret prayer, in their preaching; so little is said about secret fasting'[7] (underlining my own for emphasis).

---

[7] Jonathan Edwards, quoted in *Hunger for God,* John Piper, p.111.

My wife was recently (at the time of writing) on an extended fast of forty days, and, during this time, she visited a believer in our local area. This lady had been in church for decades and was now well into her old age. She knew that my wife was on this fast, and confessed to her that she had never fasted once in her entire life!

However, as I said in chapter 6, **if we are to grow in the spiritual life as we should, it is important for us to learn to live and walk as Jesus did, in his <u>total</u> life.** The regular practice of spiritual disciplines, **including fasting**, was the source of the inner peace, strength and spiritual power that Jesus needed in order to live and minister in the world of his day. This oft-neglected discipline of fasting was regularly practised by believers in the Bible, and Jesus assumed that his followers would also learn to practise it in their lives: he said, *'**When** you fast...'* rather than *'**If** you fast...'* (Matt. 6:16). Scripture highlights the importance of fasting by relating several examples of occasions when people fasted. For example, Queen Esther and the Jews in Susa fasted for three days and nights, praying for God to deliver his people (Esther 5:15-16). Jesus himself fasted for forty days and nights before he began his ministry (Matt. 4:2). The early apostles also fasted in order to spend time worshipping and waiting on God together (Acts 13:1-3).

Similarly, there have been many figures in the history of the Church who practised regular fasting. John Wesley, the founder of the Methodist movement, expected his preachers to fast twice a week. David Brainerd, a well-known American missionary who ministered among the indigenous people of his land, recorded in his *Diary* that he regularly set aside days (often once every week) for fasting and prayer in his ministry. John Hyde, an American missionary to India and better known as 'Praying Hyde,' often spent extended periods of time in fasting and prayer.

What is fasting?

A good definition of fasting might be: 'The choice to stay away from non-essentials for a set period of time in order to focus on what is essential.' There are various forms of fasting: we can fast from food (and perhaps also from water for short periods); from watching television and playing with computer games and gadgets (in order to quieten our minds from noise and distractions); from being with other people (in order to be on our own with God); from sexual relations with our spouse for a time (in order to concentrate on prayer, 1 Cor. 7:5); from sleeping for a few hours (in order to pray during the night; this is called 'watching'), and so on. Of these, fasting from food is perhaps the most obvious and well-known form.

As believers, we practise fasting primarily in order that we can focus on our spiritual life, on prayer and on seeking God (particularly if we have a need to get answers to specific prayers). As a by-product, it helps us to not get too wrapped up in ourselves and our material comforts, and it also helps us to keep our bodily appetites in check. Fasting for a time from gadgets and social media helps us to not become psychologically addicted to them.

It is important to understand that in fasting we are not simply keeping religious traditions. In Isaiah 58:2-9, God told the Israelites that he did not think very much of their religious fasting, and he corrected their perceptions of it. The Pharisees in Jesus' day fasted twice a week (Luke 18:11-12) and yet many of them did it hypocritically (Matt. 6:16). Furthermore, in fasting neither are we attempting to manipulate God into doing something for us; God cannot be manipulated. **The primary principle in fasting is that it enables us to get away from all distractions and to focus on our spiritual life and on specific prayers. This creates a greater penetrative power to our prayers, enabling the Holy Spirit within us to break through and overcome Satan's power**: *'you have overcome..., because the one who is in you is greater than the one who is in the world'* (1 John 4:4).

Some of the main benefits of fasting

Fasting is not an easy discipline to learn, yet it yields many benefits to those who would practise it.

a. When combined with solitude and prayer, fasting strengthens our spiritual life. It helps us to concentrate on our relationship with God and to focus our desires and prayer requests.

b. As a result of this, it helps us to become more spiritually sensitive to the Lord and brings about a greater power in our lives to combat and overcome the forces of Satan.

c. There are occasions recorded in Scripture when corporate prayer and fasting yielded answers to prayer, that prayer alone without fasting did not yield (see Judges 20:18,23,26; 2 Chron. 20:3-4ff; Mark 9:29). **It is essential that we come to understand a simple truth of spiritual life, vis. that some breakthroughs will only come about through prayer combined with fasting**. This suggests that the practice of fasting has a key place in seeing God work, in bringing victories and in seeing Satan defeated. Situations that have not previously seemed to change through prayer alone, may well change as a result of prayer and fasting.

d. Fasting also helps us to develop self-control and thereby discipline our bodily appetites. It is a medical fact that fasting for short periods of time is beneficial for our physical health.

Some advice on the practice of fasting

There is no 'one size fits all' approach to fasting. Some believers prefer to fast only occasionally, while others do it regularly as a lifestyle, often on a weekly basis. Some people fast completely from food, while others fast only partially by taking small amounts of food at intervals during the fasting period. Some do short total fasts from both food and water (but not normally going for more than three days without water). Some people do regular but short fasts, for one mealtime or for one day only, while others develop the habit of doing longer fasts for several days. Some begin their fast when they get up in the morning, others begin perhaps after lunch. Some people's working life may perhaps put limits on the length of time they can spend fasting.

With experience, we can develop our own personal pattern of fasting which we feel comfortable with. We can fast as individuals on our own, and we can also perhaps fast together corporately as a church, as we seek God for answers to specific issues.

Yonggi Cho, pastor of the largest church in the world, in South Korea, normally teaches believers to fast as a lifestyle, as an essential part of their own personal walk with God. He starts by training them first how to fast for three days, and then, having learned this, they can go on and learn how to fast for longer periods of time, such as seven or ten days. The use of Prayer Mountain in Seoul is devoted specifically to those who wish to set time apart in order to pray, fast and seek God.[8]

So, in the beginning, it is better to begin with short fasts and to slowly train yourself up into doing longer fasts, rather than simply trying to jump into the deep end of doing longer fasts straight away which might be foolhardy. **It does take time to learn the practice of fasting.** So, perhaps begin by missing one meal, then two, then go for a whole day without food, and so on. It is also probably wise to talk to someone in your church who practises fasting, so that you can benefit from their advice. **If you have any kind of ongoing medical condition or are on medicines of any sort, it is important that you seek the advice of your doctor before you embark on fasting.** It is also important to balance fasting with your working life, as fasting for longer periods can be tiring.

Perhaps the most difficult thing to overcome is our natural desire for food. Many believers confess to having had struggles in this area when first beginning to practise fasting. Perhaps the smell of food was too tempting, or, going without breakfast was easy, but missing lunch as well was simply too hard... Our physical comfort and appetites may at times get the better of our desire to pray and seek God. I am sure that many of us can relate personally to the following record of the first experience that Rees Howells, the well-known man of prayer, had of fasting:

---

[8] Cho, Paul Y., *Prayer: Key to Revival*, Word Publishing: Berkhamsted, UK, 1985, pp.103,106.

'God began to deal with a simple appetite in Rees Howells – the love of food. It was at a time when he had a great burden for a certain convention, which was being disrupted by assaults of the enemy. The Lord called him to a day of prayer and fasting, which was something new to him. Used, as he was, to a comfortable home and four good meals a day, it came as a shock to realize that it meant no dinner, and he was agitating about it. And would it only happen once? Supposing God asked him to do it every day!

When midday came he was on his knees in his bedroom, but there was no prayer that next hour. "I didn't know such a lust was in me," he said afterwards. "My agitation was the proof of the grip it had on me. If the thing had no power over me, why did I argue about it?"

At one o'clock his mother called him, and he told her he wasn't taking lunch. But she called again, as a mother would, and urged, "It won't take you long to have it." The goodly aroma from downstairs was too much for him, and down he came...'

Afterwards he confessed his disobedience and got to grips with obeying God's call to begin regularly fasting his lunch, getting victory in this area. He later recorded the following:

"'The moment I got victory in it, it wasn't a very big thing to do... It is while you still want a thing that you can't get your mind off it...'"[9]

---

[9] Taken from *Rees Howells: Intercessor*, Chapter 8 "The Tramps," by Norman Grubb, First Paperback Edition, Cambridge, UK: The Lutterworth Press, 1973, pp.58-59. Quoted by permission of The Lutterworth Press.

Going without food may well cause natural feelings of discomfort, mild headaches and perhaps even nausea during the first 24 hours, but after this time, these symptoms wear off as our bodies adjust to the fast. Perseverance begins to train our bodies and, with regular practice over a period of a few weeks, our new pattern of fasting gets established and the whole thing becomes much easier. Sometimes, when we are particularly burdened to pray, we may lose our appetite for a time and fasting comes naturally. In extended fasts, we may sometimes find ourselves becoming irritable through tiredness, especially if we have continued on with a normal daily working pattern, so we may need to ensure that we take some extra rest when we need it.

Be aware of spiritual backlash

When we begin to fast and therefore focus on seeking the Lord, meditating on Scripture and praying for specific things, not only is God aware of what we are doing, but Satan also becomes aware. He will invariably attempt to thwart our desires to gain ground for the kingdom of God, by attacking what we are doing. It is interesting that when Daniel prayed and fasted for 21 days (Dan. 10:2-3), Satanic forces tried to prevent an answer coming until the end of his fast (Dan. 10:12-13).

So when we pray and fast, we may experience spiritual backlash. This can take a multitude of different forms, such as provoking niggles in our relationship with another person or sparking off issues which may bring up past hurts; provoking changes in the attitudes and behaviour of another person towards us, or attacking the physical health of someone close to us, and so on.

When such things happen to us during a time of fasting, they can perhaps discourage us from continuing in the fast. At such times, it is important to realize that we are in a spiritual warfare (see Eph. 6:10-18) and to determine to continue in what we are doing, rather than caving in under the pressure and giving up. Through grace and perseverance, relational issues can be sorted through, healing can come, and Satan's forces can be overcome. God can bring about victories in our own life, our family, our church and our town. **Our heavenly Father, who sees what is done in secret, will indeed reward us openly** (Matt. 6:18).

Coming off a fast

When we have come to the end of our fasting period, it is wise to come off it gradually by eating only small amounts of food in the beginning, until our body gets used to taking food in again. During the fast, our stomach will have shrunk in size and our body's metabolism will have adjusted to living without regular food intake. We may be tempted to binge eat when we come off our fast, but this may lead only to our putting weight on in undesirable ways as our body stores it away. So over the first 2-3 days after the fast has ended, we should start with small amounts of food and then gradually go back to eating a normal amount over the next few days. If available, water melon is a very good way of starting to eat again after a fast.

11

ON HEALING

'I am the LORD who heals you' (Ex. 15:26)

'Heal me, O LORD, and I will be healed; save me and I will be saved, for you are the one I praise' (Jer. 17:14)

HEALING is a complex area of Christian ministry and there is probably no-one who has all the answers. However, there is much teaching in the Bible in regard to the theme of healing, and this encourages us to take a positive stance in this area. Following on from the ministries of Jesus and the early apostles, in its history the Church has practised prayer for healing as part of its regular ministry (1 Cor. 12:9-10), and there are many believers today who can testify to having experienced healing in their lives.

For many years now my wife and I have been committed to praying for believers in need of healing and freedom from spiritual oppression, and this has been part of our regular ministry wherever we have been. As a result of stepping out in faith and praying and believing for those in need, we have seen many people healed of different conditions, and these people can readily testify about what God has done in their lives. Seeing people getting healed has always been a great joy and thrill to me personally.

An example from a recent ministry appointment of how we have seen God working in answer to prayer for healing, would be the following testimony related to us by a sister in our church who was suffering from arthritis in her lower spine. She was healed in a prayer meeting led by my wife Suela in which the sick were being prayed for:

During 2009, I was suffering with a severe lower back pain which was slowly getting more painful. This had been caused by my work in a nursing home and hospital. I had got used to suffering with back pain and sciatica. I would do the usual things, like seeing my doctor and asking for prayer at church. I had also been for physiotherapy to try to get the pain sorted out, but it was not working at all.

By 2009, I was finding it difficult to bend and to get dressed, to the point where I had to ask my husband S. to help me. To stand straight was very painful and I used to count to get myself up. I continued with prayer, believing I would be healed. In September 2009, we went on a holiday to Rhodes where I took a fall and ended up with my leg in plaster and had no crutches till the following day. So I had to hop. I didn't know what hurt most, my back or my knee.

I had been recommended for a scan on my back and this identified two areas of arthritis in my spine. My doctor referred me to a pain clinic. I had spent a considerable amount of money on so-called remedies to ease the pain. As these were not working, I was offered an injection into my spine which would ease the pain for a short while.

However, on a Tuesday evening we were holding a healing prayer event in church, believing God to move powerfully for those who needed prayer. On this evening, we were praying for a lady when I could feel myself being bent over, but I was not in any pain and, in fact, seemingly bending to a degree I couldn't have managed before. I did go down in the Spirit and I knew God was healing my back. I did attend the pain clinic to explain. I was free of pain, but the doctor said I should have the injection anyway. Did I need the injection? No, God had already done the work. I thank Jesus for the healing given to me and I remain free of pain.

Some basic guidelines[10]

a. *Our belief in healing is based on God's character*

What we believe about healing is based on what we believe about God's character. God is intrinsically good and so, like any normal human parent would for their child, he desires wholeness for his people rather than sickness. Otherwise, there is no basis for a theology of healing. The Bible says that *'The LORD is gracious and compassionate, slow to anger and rich in love. The LORD is good to all; he has compassion on all he has made'* (Ps. 145:8-9).

b. *Healing demonstrates the character and the work of God*

As the Son of God, Jesus reflected God's character and therefore also his work. In the context of having healing the invalid by the pool of Bethesda, Jesus expressly stated that healing the sick was the work of the Father: *'I tell you the truth, the Son can do nothing by himself; he can only do what he sees the Father doing, because whatever the Father does the Son also does'* (John 5:17,19).

---

[10] See Blue, K. "Models of Healing", Chapter 10, *Authority to Heal.* Downers Grove, Illinois: IVP, 1987, pp.119-124.

119

Jesus demonstrated God's compassion in action by healing those who were sick: '*When Jesus landed and saw a large crowd, he had compassion on them and healed their sick*' (Matt. 14:14).

c. *Overcome the fear of failure and step out in faith*

To obtain healing, we need to be willing to take the risk of stepping out in faith and praying for it. This means, of course, that we need to be willing to become vulnerable in risking apparent failure if we do not seem to receive an answer to our prayers. Fear of failure and the consequent passivity this breeds do not see the promises of God fulfilled.

d. *Pray for healing in the name of Jesus*

So we pray to God for the sick to be healed, and we do so in the name of Jesus (see Acts 9:40, 28:8; Jas. 5:14-15). This prayer is often accompanied by the laying on of hands, but may be with or without anointing with oil.

Some common hindrances to receiving healing

a. *A wrong view of God*

Believing that God is not really a God of compassion towards you, will prevent you from believing that it is his will to heal you.

b. *Human traditions*

The teachers of Jesus' day had replaced the commandments of God with their own human traditions (Mark 7:9,13). Wrong traditions such as that God does not heal today, or that God sends sickness or that it is not God's will to heal you, will prevent you from seeking healing.

c. *Unbelief*

Jesus was unable to do any mighty miracle in his home-town of Nazareth, because the hearts of people there were full of unbelief (Mark 6:4-6). In many of the gospel accounts of healing, it is recorded that Jesus responded to people's faith in him (e.g. Matt. 8:10,13; 9:2,22).

d. *Lack of compassion*

Jesus healed because he was compassionate towards sick people (Matt. 14:14). He was deeply distressed at the hard, stubborn and uncompassionate hearts of the religious teachers of his day which prevented them from ministering healing to the sick (Mark 3:5-6).

e. *Unforgiveness*

Holding on to an attitude of unforgiveness towards those who have hurt us, prevents us from receiving any answer to our prayers (Matt. 6:14-15). The willingness to genuinely forgive is essential to receive healing.

f. *Unconfessed sin*

This will also prevent us from receiving an answer to our prayers: '*If I had cherished sin in my heart, the Lord would not have listened*' (Ps. 66:18). Sin needs to be confessed and cleansed away: '*Therefore confess your sins to each other and pray for each other so that you may be healed*' (see Jas. 5:15-16, 1 John 1:9).

g. *Lack of expectation*

The people who received healing from Jesus in the gospel accounts, came with an expectation to receive from him.

h. *Lack of perseverance*

It is through both faith <u>and</u> perseverance that we inherit the promises of God (Heb. 6:12). Perhaps our prayers sometimes do not get answered because we give up too easily when they do not seem to get answered straight away?

Three areas for healing

There are basically three areas of a person's life in which healing may be needed:

a. *Physical healing*

This is needed when our bodies are sick. Obviously, we can and should also take advantage of medical advice, medicine and / or surgery in relation to our physical condition (2 Chron. 16:12, Isa. 38:21).

b. *Inner healing of the soul*

This refers to the healing of inner emotional wounds which we may suffer from time to time. Jesus came to heal the broken-hearted (Isa. 61:1).

c. *Freedom from spiritual oppression (often called deliverance)*

This refers to being freed from the tormenting effects of an unclean spirit in a person's life. This spirit may be afflicting their inner soul or their physical body. Jesus and the apostles of the early Church cast spirits out of people on many occasions.

Meditate on the word of God to develop and strengthen your faith

Faith in our hearts removes doubt (Mark 11:22-24) and it grows and is strengthened through frequent, regular meditation on the promises of the word of God (Rom. 10:17). So one thing which we should always be encouraged to do when we are seeking healing, is to **meditate frequently and regularly on the healing promises** of the word of God: *'Do not let this book of the Law depart from your mouth; meditate on it day and night, so that you may be careful to do everything written in it. Then you will be prosperous and successful'* (Joshua 1:8 and see Ps. 1:2-3).

Below is a selection of just a few of the many passages from the Bible which speak about healing. These will help us to strengthen our faith in God's power to heal. If you are seeking healing, then meditate on them daily.

'For I am the LORD who heals you' (Ex. 15:26)

'Worship the LORD your God, and his blessing will be on your food and water. I will take away sickness from among you...' (Ex. 23:25)

*'Praise the LORD, O my soul, and forget not all his benefits –
who forgives all your sins and heals all your diseases'*
(Ps. 103:2-3)

'He sent forth his word and healed them' (Ps. 107:20)

*'No-one living in Zion will say, "I am ill"; and the sins of
those who dwell there will be forgiven'* (Isa. 33:24)

*'Surely he [Jesus] took up our infirmities and carried our
sorrows... and by his wounds we are healed'* (Isa. 53:4-5)

*'A man with leprosy came and knelt before him and said,
"Lord, if you are willing, you can make me clean." Jesus
reached out his hand and touched the man. "I am willing," he
said. "Be clean!" Immediately he was cured of his leprosy'*
(Matt. 9:2-3)

*'She said to herself, "If I only touch his cloak, I will be
healed." Jesus turned and saw her. "Take heart, daughter,"
he said, "your faith has healed you." And the woman was
healed from that moment'* (Matt. 9:21-22)

*'When Jesus had called the Twelve together, he gave them
power and authority to drive out all demons and to cure
diseases, and he sent them to preach the kingdom of God and
to heal the sick'* (Luke 9:1-2)

*'How God anointed Jesus of Nazareth with the Holy Spirit and
power, and how he went around doing good and healing all
who were under the power of the devil, because God was with
him'* (Acts 10:38)

*'And without faith it is impossible to please God, because
anyone who comes to him must believe that he exists and that
he rewards those who earnestly seek him'* (Heb. 11:6)

'Jesus Christ is the same yesterday, today and forever'
(Heb. 13:8)

'Is any one of you sick? He should call the elders of the church to pray over him and anoint him with oil in the name of the Lord. And the prayer offered in faith will make the sick person well; the Lord will raise him up. If he has sinned, he will be forgiven. Therefore, confess your sins to each other and pray for each other so that you may be healed'
(Jas. 5:14-16)

Share your testimony and pray for others in need

When we experience the healing power of God in our lives, we find it easier to then step out in faith to pray for others in need. Experiencing it for ourselves not only gives us an undeniable and living testimony, it also builds into us a deep, immovable conviction that God CAN and DESIRES to heal people and make them whole. In fact, some people who have been involved in healing ministry began their own journey in this by being healed themselves. The testimony of those who have been healed can be a tremendous encouragement to those who are sick to believe God for their own healing.

So if you have been healed, tell others of what God did for you and step out in faith and start to pray for others to be healed.

12

DEALING WITH HURTS AND INNER WOUNDS

'Get rid of all bitterness, rage... anger... and slander... forgiving
each other, just as in Christ God forgave you'
(Eph. 4:31-32)

'He heals the broken-hearted and binds up their wounds'
(Psalm 147:3)

WE have all been wounded in life to varying degrees, often in our relationships with other people. I have been hurt or wounded myself many times, even as a Christian believer and as a pastor.

In my ministry over the years, perhaps the bitterest person I have had to deal with was a lady who was then in her fifties and who had become a believer in one of the first churches I pastored. As I sat with her in her home one evening with her family present, she began to pour out many of the wounds and hurts, the disillusionment and the bitterness which had built up within her over the past several decades of her life. She seemed to me to be poisoned by bitterness. After patiently listening to her for a while, I gently broke into what she was saying and told her clearly that, to get free of her bitterness, she needed to forgive the people who had hurt her and, if possible, to get reconciled with them. She was stunned into silence by these words. Nobody had ever told her this before, and to forgive other people seemed anathema to her.

However, that evening, after talking further with her and praying together with them, she promised that she would begin this process with a particular relative in her extended family with whom she had not spoken for about twenty years. She would go, apologize and get reconciled with this person. And, what's more, she did it. She then followed this up and did it again with other people as well. It was not long before she began to be set free from the hurt and bitterness that had been rooted in her for so many years, and she became a thoroughly changed woman. She became a light for the gospel in her town and remains a stalwart member of her church to this day.

Are you wounded inside?

Inner wounds, hurts and bruises are often caused by problems in our relationships with other people, but circumstances, events and disillusionment can also give rise to such hurts. We can be wounded by people's words, by their actions towards us, by their attitudes, by breaking relationships or by things that have happened to us, and so on.

If a physical wound in our bodies remains untreated, it may continue to bleed in a specific part of our body, weakening and debilitating us. If it continues to remain untreated, infection can set in and it may go septic and fester. The infection may then spread through the body, perhaps leading ultimately to death.

There is a parallel to this with inner spiritual wounds. We are warned in Hebrews 12:15 not to allow bitterness to remain untreated, to take root and to grow up within us when we have been hurt: *'See to it that no one misses the grace of God and that no bitter root grows up to cause trouble and defile many.'* Allowing such a root to grow can turn the initial hurt and anger of the wound into resentment, rage, the poison of ongoing bitterness and even a desire for revenge.

Even though we may or may not have been at fault, or only partially so, regarding the offence done toward us, yet we often tend to make the conscious mistake of holding on to a hurt and becoming resentful, rather than seeking release from it and letting it go. So bitterness takes root, grows and begins to cause trouble.

Furthermore, in our inner hurt and anger, we often make the mistake of verbally speaking out our feelings of bitterness to other people, often slandering and cursing the character of the person who hurt us. The atmosphere around us becomes sour. The initial evil of the hurt done toward us has given rise to another evil within us, that of spreading it around amongst others. This then begins to defile or even poison their minds and hearts, and can in particular affect their own attitude towards the person who hurt us which can become warped. **In effect, we treat those around us as the rubbish bin for our own problems.** This can then lead to gossip which spreads around among the community, defiling the minds of many people.

Holding on to hurts and wounds and becoming bitter, can make our hearts become hardened (e.g. Matt. 19:8, Heb. 3:7-8), even sometimes towards God, and this can make us impervious to ministry, if we blame God for what happened. We can become tormented in our minds and memories by the wound and its associated events, often remembering every single detail, knowing no inner peace. **This root of bitterness will remain - perhaps for years - until we agree with God to deal with it properly.** It is not a rare thing to find people who are still bitter over something that happened even decades ago. Worse still, evil spirits can take advantage of our condition and gain a foothold in our life (Eph. 4:26-27), from which vantage point they can inwardly hinder our spiritual growth, continuing to torment and even bind us.

When we are bitter, we no longer relate in a healthy way to the person who hurt us, usually distancing ourselves. We may also be unable to relate effectively and maturely with other believers as well, remaining immature and unhealthy on the point on which we have been wounded because healthy spiritual growth becomes stifled. **We become chained to the problem in our past, and cannot move on in life healthy and free.**

Helpful Scriptures

There are many Bible verses that encourage us to believe that God wants to heal and free us from our inner wounds. The following verses are just some examples that we can read and meditate upon. God is a God who heals and this was exemplified especially in the ministry of Jesus which was characterized by healing people.

'...for I am the LORD, who heals you' (Ex. 15:26)

'He heals the broken-hearted and binds up their wounds' (Ps. 147:3)

'A bruised reed he will not break, and a smouldering wick he will not snuff out' (Isa. 42:3)

'He has sent me to bind up the broken-hearted... to comfort all who mourn, and provide for those who grieve... to bestow on them a crown of beauty instead of ashes, the oil of gladness instead of mourning, and a garment of praise instead of a spirit of despair'
(Isaiah 61:1-3)

'Get rid of all bitterness, rage and anger, brawling and slander, along with every kind of malice. Be kind and compassionate to one another, forgiving each other, just as in Christ God forgave you'
(Eph. 4:31-32)

Steps to inner freedom and healing

The following steps will help you to get healed and freed inwardly from your wound and its bitterness.

a. Be honest about your condition: you have a root festering within you, which is causing bondage within you and a lack of inner freedom and peace.

b. Do not continue to give in to the temptation to repay evil with evil, slandering and cursing the person or trying to take revenge (Rom. 12:17,19).

c. Stop talking about the problem to other people and expressing the bitterness that you feel (Eph. 4:29). You don't have the right to defile other people with your bitterness, anger, gossip and slandering.

d. Recall the issue. What happened? Who was the person? When did it happen? How did it happen?

131

e. Recognize and accept that God was not at fault concerning what happened. Accusing him will simply prevent you from receiving the very grace and healing power you need and that he can give you. **The problem was caused in daily living itself and probably in a relational situation.**

f. The crucial issue in the process of finding inner freedom is **not to miss God's grace** (Heb. 12:15) which is always available.

g. Open up to God about the problem, and also to your pastor who can handle your problem in a discreet and mature way (1 John 1:7).

h. Confess your need to be healed and released, and also confess your own sins in consciously holding on to the hurt and perhaps also of spreading it around among others.

i. Prayerfully, re-visit the experience and walk through it again, inviting Jesus to be present – he is eternal and was there when it happened, and he knows all about it. As you walk through it prayerfully, invite and allow him to specifically touch, cleanse, heal and free the tender, vulnerable, hurt and wounded part of you.

j. Prayerfully, take a stand of faith and command any evil spirits to depart from you, and proclaim to them that you are retaking the ground within you that they have stolen from you.

k. Prayerfully, ask God to flood you inwardly with his grace which can strengthen and save you, and can completely release you from the bondage you are in. God's grace works at a deeper level than sin and its effects within you (Rom. 5:20-21). It will heal, cleanse and free you from all the hurt, pain, anger and bitterness you feel.

l. Claim and receive the freedom and healing you need, according to the promises of God's word.

m. Agree with God that you must completely release and forgive the person or people who wounded you, <u>and do this as a conscious act of your will</u>, expressing it verbally also.

n. Begin to pray for them that God will bless them (Luke 6:28, Rom. 12:20).

Forgiveness is the key to inner healing

Jesus taught his followers to pray: *'forgive us our debts, as we forgive us debtors'* (Matt. 6:12), clearly showing that he expected that his followers would learn to forgive others. He also taught that if we will not forgive other people, then God himself will not forgive us either: with the measure we use, it will be measured to us (Matt. 6:14-15, 7:2, 18:35). The unmerciful servant took his own forgiveness for granted, but did not extend the same heart attitude of forgiveness to others who needed his forgiveness and mercy, and he paid a heavy price for this (see Matt. 18:21-35).

So our challenge in dealing with inner wounds is to imitate God (Eph. 5:1) who forgives those who sin against him: *'forgiving each other, just as in Christ God forgave you'* (Eph. 4:32). Jesus' own attitude was one of forgiveness when he prayed, *'Father, forgive them for they know not what they do'* (Luke 23:34). **Effectively, our choice is to stay as we are with our wound, staying chained to it in unforgiveness (or worse, becoming like the person who hurt us, rendering evil for evil), or to become like God and so become free.** By becoming like God, we become free ourselves (Matt. 5:48).

However, we also need to realise that releasing those who hurt us and forgiving them is not the same thing as letting them 'get off scot free.' They still have to answer to God, so we need to release them into God's hands and then let him deal with them: *'Vengeance is mine, I will repay, says the LORD'* (Rom. 12:19). However, if they repent, God will also forgive them. Forgiving the person releases the Holy Spirit to bring conviction to them, and this may then lead to repentance on their part as they realise their wrong, and it may also bring about reconciliation in our relationship with them. However, **to become free and stay free, we ourselves must forgive the person whether they repent or not.**

Forgiveness is not a matter of words, of just saying it. Forgiveness has to be from the heart: full, complete and total, in order for us to be truly healed and set free. **Genuine forgiveness simply means a willingness to fully release the person who hurt us, without holding on anymore to any of the hurt, letting it all go.** Forgiveness is a choice we make. **However, holding on to an attitude of unforgiveness simply condemns us to remaining chained to our wound from the past with all of its inward torment.**

Go through the steps to freedom listed above as many times as you need until inward release and freedom come. It may be necessary with deep or longstanding wounds to go through these steps several times, and full release may not come about for some time, but perseverance will indeed bring about the freedom you need, if you are willing to completely forgive.

13

OVERCOMING OUR INWARD SHAME

'...and they hid from the LORD God among the trees of the garden'
(Gen. 3:8)

'Search me, O God, and know my heart; test me and know my anxious thoughts. See if there is any offensive way in me, and lead me in the way everlasting' (Ps. 139:23-24)

Reading: Genesis 3:1-21

In hiding

WHEN God looked for Adam and his wife in the garden after they had disobeyed him, to walk with them and to enjoy fellowship with them, he found that they had hidden themselves from him. Their sin had produced fear, shame and feelings of guilt within them, so their reaction was to run away from God and to try to hide themselves: *'I heard you... I was afraid... so I hid'* (Gen. 3:10). They could not face God, so they tried to hide their sin, out of fear that it would be exposed, and that they might be rejected and judged. They understood that they had a problem and they tried to cover up the outward physical shame of nakedness with fig-leaves, but the real problem was within their hearts, of course. **Sin produces feelings of**

guilt and inward shame in our hearts and, as a result, we try to cover it up, being afraid to face our real inward selves and God.

There are other examples in the Scriptures in which we can perhaps discern this sense of inward shame. When King David became aware that his sinful liaison with Bathsheba had led to her becoming pregnant, he tried to cover his sin up by committing another sin against her husband Uriah (2 Sam. 11). The prodigal expressed his sense of shame at his wilfulness and profligate conduct with his words: *'I have sinned against heaven and against you. I am no longer worthy to be called your son'* (Luke 15:21). Peter's open denial of Christ three times caused him to go outside and weep bitterly (Luke 22:54-62), feeling ashamed at himself for not standing faithfully by Jesus, and so on.

The inward shame caused by ways in which we may have lived, behaved, spoken and conducted ourselves – or the consequences of such – and any associated feelings of guilt, can cause us to respond much as Adam and his wife did: we bury things deep within our hearts and cover them up for fear of being known for who and what we really are. We avoid the embarrassment and humiliation which would be caused by open exposure of shame hidden within. So our points of shame become our inward secrets, known only to ourselves, hidden behind a veil deep within. **We hide our real inward self.**

The obsession with outward image in westernized societies can sometimes – but not always – be simply a mask to cover over deep inward insecurity as people cannot face their real selves within. Adam and his wife covered themselves up with fig-leaves so as not to be exposed (Gen. 3:7), and we too can use many kinds of figurative fig-leaves to cover up our real inward self. We can simply deny that we have such inner problems; we can build a wall of protection around ourselves that no-one can penetrate; we can overdress or dress in strange ways, seeking for acceptance through our outward image; we can try to be someone that we are not, trying to be like others, so wearing a mask; we may become a perfectionist, being overly competitive or having a critical or arrogant spirit towards others; our inward insecurity can cause us to chase worldly success, thinking that through this we will be accepted by others, and so on. However, **regardless of any outward covering, a person is what they are in their hearts**: as a man thinks in his heart, so is he (Prov. 23:7). We <u>are</u> our secrets![11]

The crippling effects of inward shame

Inward shame can be caused in many different ways: perhaps a problem with alcohol, drugs or pornography which was rooted in deep, unhealed pain within; perhaps a problem with gambling which caused divisions within your marriage or family; perhaps the guilt and shame associated with abortion; perhaps inappropriate sexual activity or an ongoing problem with lust and pornography; perhaps the pain of a divorce which was accompanied by nasty infighting between you and your spouse; perhaps the shame of a prison record and what brought it about; perhaps simply a memory of something which happened many years ago, the pain of which still torments you, and so on. Abuse in childhood (for which you were not guilty) causes deep unresolved feelings of shame which can bring about inward torment stretching well into adult years.

---

[11] Bradshaw, J. *Healing the Shame that Binds You*, Deerfield Beach: Health Communications, 1988.

The effects of inward shame caused by sin can be spiritually crippling and can bind us. Hiding things deep within, because we do not want to be known by others on those points, only causes us to isolate ourselves. Such isolation then makes us easy targets for Satan, the accuser, who delights to prey on areas of inward shame and to torment us with thoughts that we can never get free of this thing, or be wanted, accepted or forgiven by God or worthy of his love, or accepted by others (cf. Zech. 3:1).

So we can end up becoming the despairing victims of ongoing, unseen, inward torment. We cannot face or forgive ourselves, and we do not open up to others out of fear of their scrutiny, as they might simply judge, criticize and perhaps gossip about us. We are isolated within, bound to the memory of the shame. We do not grow beyond it and are not released from it to serve God in real freedom. In our inward dysfunctionality, we end up struggling with a toxic mixture of shame, fear, guilt, embarrassment, self-rejection and the fear or assumption of being rejected by others and by God, perhaps even thinking that there is something defective about us as a person.

Furthermore, it may well be true that if we opened up and shared an area of inward shame with some kinds of religious people, hoping for their help, then, rather than responding with an attitude which reflects the grace and love of God and which can help in setting us free, they might react with a judgemental or critical attitude. This then only compounds the shame we feel and keeps us captive to it, so making it even harder for us to open up again.

The shame of the cross

In order to deal with Adam and his wife's inner problem, **God exposed it in grace and love**. Although there were consequences for them after their fall, yet God did not reject them, and he gave them garments of skin to be clothed with, to replace the fig-leaves they had made for themselves (Gen. 3:21). The fig-leaves were not enough to remove the real inner problem of sin and shame (cf. Isa. 28:20). God provided for them a better covering through the shedding of blood. This points to the forgiveness, redemption and righteousness made available through the shedding of Christ's blood (Eph. 1:7 and cf. Rev. 6:11; 7:9,13-14). However we try to cover up our inner problems, it is no use before God. He can see through to our hearts and can see what lies within us, but he has also provided the way for us to be forgiven and cleansed deep within, and to be truly freed and released from our sin and shame (Rev. 1:5b).

When Jesus was crucified on the cross, he bore ALL our sins, so that God could bring forgiveness to anyone who accepts his saving work. However, what is not often emphasized is that **his atoning work on the cross also deals with our deep, inward shame.** Jesus was crucified naked, in public, outside the city on a hillside where everyone could see (Heb. 13:13). In this open, public exposure, he experienced the intense, inward agony of what it was to feel shamed, mocked and humiliated. He was not able to hide. He was openly *'despised and rejected by men, a man of sorrows and familiar with suffering'* (Isa. 53:3). **So in his atoning work he knew and identified with shame:** *'he endured the cross, scorning the shame'* (Heb. 12:2).

Hence, when we come to Jesus, we come to one who, although he was without sin himself, yet he understands our own deep, inward feelings of shame, and so in grace he can reach down into the deepest points of our shame and heal us right there, forgiving us for whatever caused the shame, and freeing us from the binding effects it has on us. **In his grace, his own open exposure in shame brings us inward healing.**

The deep, deep love of Jesus

In marriage, a husband and wife are *'naked, and not ashamed'* (Gen. 2:25). Being married is to know another person and to be known by them, imperfectly yet deeply and intimately, in that which we are and do, and yet still to know their love and their embrace of acceptance in spite of our weaknesses and failures.

In a similar way also, in our relationship with God, we stand naked before him and are known deeply and intimately by him in the very depths of our heart and our being. The most inward parts of our life, where the deepest secrets are held, are unfolded to him. God knows us through and through. He knows the secrets of our hearts: *'For the word of God is living... piercing even to the dividing of soul and spirit... quick to discern the thoughts and intents of the heart... all things are naked and laid open before the eyes of him with whom we have to do'* (Heb. 4:12-13), and *'O LORD, you have searched me and you know me'* (Ps. 139:1).

However, God does not simply <u>know</u> what we are deep down inside, **he also loves us even more deeply.** In our shame, we find it easy to believe that he might reject us, but actually his grace and love for us are unconditional, never-ending and indeed extravagant. Jesus took ALL our sins upon himself on the cross. **Our points of shame are precisely the places in our life that God would want us to**

open up to him, so that he can lavish his grace, love, acceptance, cleansing and healing of us on these points. Our shame does not cause him to reject us; he is not offended by the symptoms. Binding up the broken-hearted was why Jesus came (Isa. 61:1). So he accepts us and yearns for us to be healed and set free from our shame and from the effects it has had on us, to then be able to walk in deep, inward assurance of his everlasting love and acceptance of us. He is <u>FOR</u> us: *'The LORD your God is with you, he is mighty to save. He will take great delight in you, he will quiet you with his love, he will rejoice over you with singing'* (Zeph. 3:17).

This deep love of God, by which we are brought into freedom before him, removing our sense of shame, can again be discerned in many examples in Scripture. The prodigal was received back with compassion, he was forgiven and clothed, and there was a feast for him. After his denials, Peter was re-commissioned in mercy and love (John 21:15-19). The unknown, sinful woman who anointed Jesus' feet in Simon the Pharisee's house, was very aware within herself of Jesus' forgiveness and she responded with deep love for him, and was sent away in peace (Luke 7:36-50). When she was brought to Jesus, the woman caught in adultery found herself with no accusers, and was not condemned by Jesus, but was told to go and sin no more (John 8:3-11), and so on.

Hindrances to coming out of hiding

So if there is healing for us when we are willing to come out of hiding, then we need to deal with those particular hindrances which may prevent us from coming out of hiding and opening up (cf. John 3:19-21).

Firstly, with God, **there is no fear in exposure.** Our tendency might be to not believe that God still loves us utterly, when it becomes clear to us that he both sees and knows our areas of shame. So we may make the mistake of trying to keep our shame 'in hiding,' and, as a result, we remain as we are. However, *'there is no fear in love. But perfect love drives out fear, because fear has to do with punishment. The one who fears is not made perfect in love'* (1 John 4:18). God IS love (1 John 4:8,16). A believer who fears rejection by God simply does not yet understand God's love well enough to know that s/he truly is forgiven and can be set completely free. God has not given us the spirit of fear, but the spirit of love (2 Tim. 1:7 AV), so if we are willing to face ourselves as God sees us and open ourselves up to him on these points, then we can experience his love and compassion in healing and releasing us from shame.

Secondly, there may also be **a tendency to feel guilty and to condemn ourselves.** However, again, grasping the depth of God's love for us will help us to overcome this. Jesus took God's judgement on sin in our place on the cross, so we are accepted in Christ, the Beloved, and freed from guilt (Eph. 1:6 AV). The blood of Jesus cleanses us from ALL sin (1 John 1:7) and it deals effectively with the inward parts of our life: it cleanses our heart and frees our conscience from guilt (Heb. 9:14, 10:22). So **we should learn to forgive ourselves just as God himself has forgiven us. God's love brings acceptance and healing.** Condemning ourselves locks us out from knowing God's love and healing, and simply allows the devil to continue to accuse and torment us within. *'Therefore, there is now no condemnation for those who are in Christ Jesus... Who shall separate us from the love of Christ?'* (Rom. 8:1,35). Receiving God's love for us is the key to getting release from being captives to inward torment; it disempowers Satan.

Thirdly, **our pride may prevent us from coming humbly to receive God's love to cleanse and free us within**, not wanting to confess and expose our shame to him. However, God's grace is given to those who humble themselves; he resists the proud (1 Peter 5:5). Pride closes the door on becoming free and rejoicing in God's love for us.

Steps to inner freedom and healing

Humbling ourselves and opening up our area of shame to God, allows him to touch us deeply and free us at that point with his grace, love, acceptance and healing. When we are inwardly freed from our shame and torment, resting in his love for us, we can begin to love ourselves just as God loves us. We can confidently but humbly lift our head and our heart high, resting in the deep, inward assurance that we have been freed and that we stand clean and totally accepted before God. We can be our real selves again, no longer needing any proverbial fig-leaves to cover ourselves up and hide our real selves from others. We can face our accuser and tell him that everything really has been cleansed away and is under the blood of Jesus, and that the accuser of the brethren has been cast down (Rev. 12:10). God rebukes our accuser, takes off our filthy clothes, takes away our sin, places new, rich garments on us and re-commissions us in his work (Zech. 3:1-7). We are free to confidently and boldly proclaim the love and restoring power of God to others who face similar issues of shame and guilt.

The steps to inner freedom and healing from areas of inward shame are very similar to those outlined in chapter 12 on inner hurts and wounds, and you could perhaps read those through again at this point.

a. Face the area of shame, and open it up to God through prayer and confession, bringing it into the light together with any sin associated with it. It might be beneficial to open up also to your pastor, who will be able to help you with counsel in discretion and maturity. *'If we walk in the light, as he is in the light, we have fellowship with one another, and the blood of Jesus, his Son, purifies us from all sin... If we confess our sins, he is faithful and just and will forgive us our sins and purify us from all unrighteousness'* (1 John 1:7,9).

b. Risking such exposure of your area of shame will make you feel vulnerable, at least initially. **However, this will lead to experiencing God's acceptance and love, not his rejection**, and this will help you to change any wrong patterns of thinking that you may have developed about yourself.

c. Prayerfully, re-visit the experience and walk through it again, inviting Jesus to be present – he is eternal and was there when it happened, and he knows all about it. As you walk through it prayerfully, invite and allow him to specifically heal and free the tender and vulnerable part of you.

d. Receive the love of God for you and the embrace of his forgiveness. Pray for and receive complete healing in this area of your life.

e. Forgive yourself for any sin associated with this area of shame, and enjoy the restoration of joy, hope and freedom in your heart.

f. Take a stand of faith and command any tormenting evil spirits to depart from you.

g. Completely release and forgive any person or people who were involved in your life concerning the area of shame.

h. Learn to love yourself just as God loves you. Be your real self again.

i. Whenever you need to, tell the accuser that everything has been cleansed away and is under the blood of Christ, and that he has been cast down.

j. As a precaution, once you have experienced the grace and love of God in healing and cleansing away your area of shame, it is perhaps wise not to simply go out and start telling everyone about the details of it. Not all people will be mature enough to handle the weight of what you are saying, and may still simply judge or criticize you, or gossip about what you have told them, and this might then make you feel hurt or rejected again.

If shame gets hidden in the intimacy of our hearts, then healing from shame is also an intimate ministry. What has been ministered in intimacy then needs to be handled wisely before other people. Testimony can and should indeed be given to bring glory to God, but not all the details need to be shared or should be shared, except with those whom we know can handle what they hear with wisdom, discretion and maturity.

14

WALKING IN HOLINESS

'Be holy because I, the LORD your God, am holy' (Lev. 19:2)

'...for the prince of this world is coming. He has no hold on me...'
(John 14:30 NIV)

'...for the prince of the world cometh: and he hath nothing in me'
(John 14:30 AV)

Reading: 2 Samuel chs. 11-12

Don't give the devil a foothold

THE sorry tale of king David's sin with Bathsheba serves to illustrate the potential consequences of sexual sin. It is a warning to us all (1 Cor. 10:11). The unwillingness to control himself, flirting with and entertaining sinful desires in his heart and mind, and yielding to a deceptive temptation in a moment of vulnerability, marked a turning point in David's life and led to unforeseen and tragic consequences for all concerned, especially David's family. **The passion of uncontrolled sinful desire caused him to lose perspective on the potential consequences of sin.** The heart is indeed deceitful above all things...

In the words of Ephesians 4:27, David 'gave the devil a foothold' in his life. These words show us that Satan can gain access into our lives through sin, and they suggest pointedly to us that we should not play with sin or take it lightly. If we do, Satan will never be far away from getting an open door into our life, making it easier for him to bring about a time and place of temptation, or to throw his fiery darts into us (Eph. 6:16).

In order to cover up the fact that it was he who had made Bathsheba pregnant, David hatched a deceptive plan involving her loyal husband Uriah (which failed), and afterwards arranged for him to be killed on the battlefield. David then married his pregnant widow, adding further to his polygamous household. **Entertaining sin in his life empowered Satan against David, allowing Satan's influence to gain a foothold in his life to trap him. This then began to influence, trap and destroy others through him.**

When his sin was uncovered to him by Nathan the prophet, David was conscience-stricken and Psalm 51 records his genuine repentance. However, although God was gracious enough to forgive him, David still had to face the ongoing consequences of his actions; he was not absolved of these. **Giving place to sin in our life has a ripple effect: it first affects our own personal lives, and then, through us, it can then begin to affect those close to us, and then yet others.** We reap what we have sown. Our negative example is empowered to affect our children and other people. If the devil can get a foothold in our life, then he has got into our marriage and our home and he will then try to go a step further and get into our children's lives also. **If this is not dealt with thoroughly through repentance, it can then potentially lead to a generational pattern of 'steal, kill and destroy' down through our family-tree** (John

10:10). **A foothold in our life which is undealt with, may eventually also become a stronghold and then a stranglehold in its varying degrees of destructive influence.**

Nathan's prophetic words to David that the sword would never depart from his house and that calamity would come upon him out of his own household, must have been crushing. The child of the adulterous liaison died soon after he was born and David's family life was never the same again; everything went downhill from that point onwards.

In addition to his polygamy, the father's negative example of sexual sin bred sexual sin in his children, and murder bred murder. The narrative goes on to record in subsequent chapters that David's son Amnon raped his half-sister Tamar whose brother Absalom then took revenge and murdered Amnon. Absalom later conspired against his father David and dishonoured him by lying with his father's concubines in broad daylight, but was killed in the civil war that resulted from his conspiracy. Adonijah thought he had a right to the throne and rebelled against Solomon, Bathsheba's son, and he too was murdered. **Sin exacts its price from us, and the all-round price that David paid for his sin was bitter indeed** (Rom. 6:23), **a real unholy mess in his family which, in his case, he could never put right.**

What is holiness?

This sobering example of David's sin and its tragic consequences underlines to us the importance of walking in holiness in our lives.

151

The Hebrew word *qadash* (meaning 'to make holy' or 'to sanctify') seems to be related to the concepts of both purity and separation, and expresses the idea of being consecrated to God for his use. Similarly, the Greek word *hagios* (meaning 'holy') primarily expresses the idea of separation, and in particular to be separated or set aside from ordinary use, in order to be used for sacred purposes. It is also used to convey the concept of the work of the Holy Spirit within us as believers to produce the subjective, inward quality of holiness. So the concept of holiness brings together the two related issues of our inward, spiritual condition and our usefulness to God in his purposes for us. It has the negative aspect of separation FROM sin, and the positive aspects of inward purity and separation UNTO God for his use.

The exhortation to the Israelites as God's people to *'Be holy, for I am holy'* (Lev. 11:44-45; 19:2; 20:7,26) was repeated to Christians by the apostle Peter (1 Peter 1:14-16). For the early Israelites, the exhortation was to separate themselves from the sexual, moral and idolatrous practices of the Canaanites and the Egyptians (see Lev. 18), and so to steer clear of the spiritual bondages which these practices caused. Similarly, for the early Christians, the exhortation was to separate themselves from the kind of sinful desires and lifestyles common in the Greco-Roman world in which they lived, that would have characterized many of them prior to their becoming believers, and to live in accordance with the principles of God's word.

However, the Israelites found difficult this call to be 'separated out,' to be willing to be consciously different in the way in which they lived their lives, and the Old Testament narrative informs us that, as a nation, they compromised time after time, falling into spiritual bondage and the oppression which came about as a direct consequence. **It seems that many times they simply could not bear to be different.** Not only did they find it too challenging to live differently to those around them, they also did not seem to get to grips with the concept that God was calling them to be separated from sinful lifestyles and separated unto God as his people, specifically in order that they might then become a witness to the surrounding nations as God's priestly nation in this world (cf. Ex. 19:5-6). The point was not merely to be different, it was so that they could then fulfil God's purpose for them as a nation. **Their difficulty in accepting to be different, caused them to miss out on God's purpose for themselves.**

Living out of inward empowerment, not religious legalism

In the Old Testament, the call to live a holy life was a command and an exhortation. However, because of our sinful inward natures, any human attempt to match up to a particular standard of holy living, inevitably leads to the frustration of religious legalism. **We try, but we cannot do it, so we end up wearing a religious mask to cover up the real, inward state of our hearts.** This inward frustration would have been part of the Israelites' experience, as is made clear to us by the apostle Paul (Rom. 7:7-25). However, as Christian believers living in the new covenant, we are not expected to live up to any standard of holiness merely by our own human weakness or effort. **We have been given the inward empowering of the Holy Spirit to help us to walk freely in holiness:** *'live by the Spirit, and you will not gratify the desires of the sinful nature'* (Gal. 5:16; Rom. 8:2-3,6).

God is intrinsically holy in his nature (Lev. 11:44-45, 19:2). He is light and there is no darkness in him at all (1 John 1:5). His call to us to 'be holy, for I am holy' is a command and an exhortation, but it is also an encouragement and an invitation to cooperate with the Holy Spirit in his purpose of making us holy. So this inward process of sanctification, of becoming internally holy, should never be confused with the controlling legalism which is characteristic of religious living. It is the natural outworking of what it means to be born-again and to be filled with and walk in the presence and power of the Holy Spirit (cf. 1 Peter 2:2, 2 Peter 3:18). The growth of inward holiness is a progressive work within us which is done by the Holy Spirit **as we learn to walk with and to cooperate with him.** The Holy Spirit makes us like himself; progressively he makes us internally clean, pure and holy (Lev. 20:8, 22:32).

This does not mean that we become intrinsically perfect or inwardly sinless at any stage (1 John 1:8). It means that we continue to be 'a work in progress' and are being progressively freed and purified from the control of sinful tendencies within us (Rom. 6:14), particularly in terms of what were once habitual sins in our lives (1 John 3:9). The call to holiness is an invitation to learn to become progressively more like God as his children, subjectively as an inward process, and then in terms of how we live and are used by God. We can see this call to become like God in other areas too, for example in terms of the practical operation of God's overcoming grace through us as believers (see Matt. 5:43-48, Luke 6:27-36) and in terms of giving forgiveness to others (Eph. 4:32 - 5:1). **As we become progressively more holy, then God is making us more and more like himself.**

So the key factor in this issue of inward sanctification (and also of being used by God) **is our relationship with the Holy Spirit as he continues to abide within us.** Influence has effects. So, if the influence of bad company is to corrupt good character (1 Cor. 15:33), then, by contrast, learning to live consistently in the presence of the Holy Spirit, will produce the fruit of holiness in our lives which is *'righteousness, peace and joy in the Holy Spirit'* (Rom. 14:17). We must learn to walk consistently in his presence and in his empowerment in our lives. **The influence of his pervasive holy presence makes us holy; his purity makes us pure.**

Both Andrew Murray and Charles Spurgeon underlined this need to walk consistently in the presence of God when they said the following: 'Nowhere can we get to know the holiness of God, and come under His influence and power, except in the inner chamber. It has been well said: "No man can expect to make progress in holiness who is not often and long alone with God"' (Andrew Murray), and, 'If you think you can walk in holiness without keeping up perpetual fellowship with Christ, you have made a great mistake. If you would be holy, you must live close to Jesus' (Charles Spurgeon).[12]

That Christ died to sin in order that we too may die to it and be raised with him into newness of life, is the plain teaching of Romans 6; sin will not have dominion over us (Rom. 6:14). We overcome the bias of the gravitational pull of sin in our lives, by setting into motion another, more powerful force, that of the presence and power of the Holy Spirit. We cannot overcome sin in our own strength, any more than a Saturn V rocket can escape the earth's gravity without the

---

[12] Taken from http://christian-quotes.ochristian.com, accessed 06-01-2015.

power of its engines. So a key question then is: what will help us to maintain closeness in our fellowship with the Holy Spirit and see his presence and power released in our lives?

However, although we need to be clear on the issue of what it means to live a Spirit-filled and Spirit-empowered life, yet seeking a once-for-all experience of his presence and power will not suffice us to walk in holiness over a lifetime. In addition to learning to live a life filled with his presence, perhaps the answer to the issue of holiness lies also in considering the all-round practice of a complex of biblical concepts such as understanding true repentance as learning to think the way God does, and so walking in the transformation of the renewing of our minds (Rom. 12:2); walking in the daily confession of sin and its cleansing (1 John 1:7-9); knowing the word of God, internalizing its principles (Ps. 119:11), and walking in obedience to as much of it as we have presently understood (John 8:31-32); gaining freedom from any particular oppressive spirits which may be working in our lives (Isa. 61:1); learning how to recognize a time and place of temptation for what it is when it is coming our way, and handling it with integrity, wisdom and courage (1 Cor. 10:13); regularly practising basic spiritual disciplines; walking in a spirit of free praise, and taking the time necessary to devotionally seek and walk in the presence and power of the Holy Spirit, and so on.

Holiness as wholeness, freedom and order

So holiness is not a dull, boring, negative, controlling, 'religious' concept which takes the enjoyment out of daily life. **It is essentially a positive concept.** A person who lives in holiness is a truly free and happy person.

The picture given in Scripture of a maturing believer is one of freedom: *'if the Son sets you free, you will be free indeed'* (John 8:36) and *'you will know the truth, and the truth will set you free'* (John 8:32); *'sin shall not be your master,'* it *'shall not have dominion over you'* (Rom. 6:14 AV and NIV); *'the mind controlled by the Spirit is life and peace'* (Rom. 8:6), and so on.

In contrast to this state of freedom and peace, is the person who does not live and walk in holiness, who lives in sin or in spiritually immature carnality (cf. 1 Cor. 3:1-3). Because such a person has not yet understood their true identity in Christ as a 'holy one' or 'saint' and that his/her call in him is to be holy (cf. 1 Cor. 1:2 etc.) and therefore does not yet appreciate the need to walk in holiness, s/he remains a slave to sin (cf. John 8:34), simply submitting him/herself with no real, inward freedom to do what pleases the carnal nature. Such a person often confuses liberty (the choice to do what I want regardless of the consequences) with freedom (the ability to say 'No' to whatever may bring me into enslavement).

A key to walking in holiness, as Paul told the Corinthians, is that **we become what we are in Christ and therefore walk *'as [we] really are'*** (1 Cor. 5:7). Knowing who we really are, and seeing ourselves as new creations in Christ (2 Cor. 5:17), is an encouragement to *'get rid of the old yeast'* (1 Cor. 5:7). This means agreeing with God to repent of and forsake the sins of our past, and recognizing, confessing and dealing with any sins in the present. The blood of Jesus purifies us and frees us from all our sins (1 John 1:9, Rev. 1:5b). **It is axiomatic that we cannot walk in holiness and freedom, if we have any unconfessed sins in our life.** Sin grieves the Holy Spirit within us (Eph. 4:29-31).

157

Furthermore, from a pastoral perspective, it is also good for believers to learn to catch and deal with issues in the beginning, rather than struggling inwardly as an individual and seeking counsel only afterwards when any damage is already done. When struggling with issues of sin in our life, learning to be accountable is good for us. God has given us ministers as parents in the faith (1 Cor. 4:15; Eph. 4:11-16; 1 Thess. 2:7,11-12). As believers, we should learn not to be so very private that we isolate ourselves in dealing with our issues. This only leads into the inevitable vicious circle of struggling with sin and not being able to overcome it.

Another key to walking in holiness is **walking in the transformation brought about by the renewing of our minds** (Rom. 12:2). The essence of a renewed mind and a renewed way of thinking is seeing and understanding things from God's perspective. This is what Paul meant by having *'the mind of Christ'* (1 Cor. 2:16). In a nutshell, it means to no longer think according to the way the world thinks, or to value what it values, but to know what God thinks about any given thing and to live in accordance with that: *'those who live in accordance with the Spirit have their minds set on what the Spirit desires'* (Rom. 8:5). So, with a renewed mind, we learn to think about *'whatever is true, whatever is noble, whatever is right, whatever is pure, whatever is lovely, whatever is admirable,'* and whatever is excellent or praiseworthy (Phil. 4:8). This then helps us understand why walking in holiness is good and beneficial for us. It also helps us to maintain holiness in our minds and our lives, and we then also make right choices.

An important expression of holiness is that of **inward, spiritual wholeness**, meaning freedom from any inward spiritual torment or oppression. Such spiritual bondage enslaves a person, but Jesus came to set the captives free (Isa. 61:1). Until a person has gained their freedom in Christ from any such spiritual oppression or inward torment, they are not free to be as God would have them be and to serve him in true freedom, but remain chained to their particular inward issue(s). Evil spirits, regardless of the cause which brought about their entanglement in a person's life, always oppress, enslave, torment and defile a person. They need to be dealt with through the authority of Christ, and cast out. We need to deal with any potential or actual footholds evil spirits may have within us. The ground within us on which they may work, and the entrance point they may have used in the past, need to be addressed and dealt with appropriately.

It is also important to deal with issues such as bitterness, anger, unforgiveness, inner hurts and wounds, and so on (Eph. 4:31-32), as these bring about inward spiritual bondage which can last for years, in fact until they are dealt with properly. It is in the context of undealt-with anger that Paul said 'do not give the devil a foothold' (Eph. 4:26-27). Similarly, undealt-with issues of inward shame and guilt can become entrance points for the devil to oppress and torment a person.

Bearing in mind the tragic example of king David, it is also important to realize that, although confession and genuine repentance from sin bring God's cleansing and forgiveness, and although this then closes the door on the effects of that particular sin in our own personal life, yet Satan can still work through the damage that our sin may have caused in other people. If our sin has released bitterness or even demonic activity in our home, then it is likely that our children may become embittered or under the influence of that demonic activity in their own lives, and perhaps so on generationally. These people will themselves then have to deal redemptively with the consequences and effects of our sin upon their own lives. In order for them to be able to re-build their future, it may be necessary for us to apologize and seek forgiveness from those so affected.

Another expression of holiness is **freedom from any and all things which can enslave a person, spiritually, psychologically or physically. True holiness means freedom, and true freedom is only found in holiness.** So it is important for believers to aim to get free and remain free of any dependency on, or addiction to, substances, drugs, smoking, alcohol, involvement in the occult, pornography, and so on. These things can all enslave a person, and such an enslaved person is not yet truly free in Christ.

In a word, holiness brings about **order and a state of inward orderliness** in a person's life. The person is free, can learn to live in freedom and can enjoy the positive fruit of remaining free to love and serve God. Thereafter, a key issue in maintaining our walk in holiness, is doing whatever we need to do to maintain our spiritual freedom.

Honouring God: wanting to please him

Loving God and desiring his presence in our lives will naturally make us want to please him. Desiring to honour God and to honour our relationship with him in our life, should lead to freely and willingly choosing to do what we know would please him. We should *'find out what pleases the Lord'* (Eph. 5:10) and live accordingly. Holiness is choosing to live as God would live. **As his children, we should imitate our Father** (Eph. 5:1) **and choose to**

be holy, because we want to be like him (Lev. 19:2, 1 Peter 1:15-16).

For example, we should choose to honour God with our bodies as these are the temples in which the Holy Spirit lives (1 Cor. 6:19-20), and not yield to any desire or temptation to use them for sexual immorality, as this would grieve him. **Understanding that we have been redeemed should lead into the decision to honour God** (1 Cor. 6:18-20), so we should offer our bodies as servants of righteousness leading to holiness (Rom. 6:19-23, 1 Thess. 4:3-8, 1 Peter 4:3-6). We walk in holiness because we love God, because we fear him, because we want to please him, because we want to see him, and because we want to be like him. David expressed such a desire when he prayed: *'Give me an undivided heart, that I may fear your name'* (Ps. 86:11). We learn to resist sin, because we understand that God is training us into a lifestyle of holiness which produces a harvest of righteousness and peace (Heb. 12:4-14).

In addition to king David's failure, Scripture also records the case of Samson who played fast and loose with his divine calling, and paid a heavy price for his love of Philistine women (see Judges chs. 13-16). However, where Samson and king David both failed, Joseph succeeded (see Gen. 39:6-20). Faced with the pressure of manipulative and repeated temptation, he eventually fled the scene (and later faced the unjust consequences of his wise choice). However, the heart of Joseph's response in overcoming this temptation is found in his words *'How could I do such a thing and sin against God?'* (Gen. 39:9). For him, the issue was not simply whether he should betray Potiphar's trust and have an illicit sexual relationship with his wife, but whether he should still choose to honour God and so do the right thing, regardless of the temptation he faced. **Joseph chose to not compromise. He did not give in to temptation and enjoy sin, because he wanted to honour and please God. He won his internal battle over his moral integrity.**

In addition to wanting to please him, another strong reason for living and walking in holiness as believers is **the fear of God**, that we will one day face the judgement seat of Christ, to answer for the deeds done while in the body (2 Cor. 5:9-10). Sexual immorality in particular is associated in several passages of the New Testament with the judgement of God (see 1 Cor. 6:9-10, 1 Thess. 4:3-8, Heb. 12:14-16, 1 Peter 4:3-5). As the book of Proverbs teaches us, the beginning of wisdom is walking in the fear of God (Prov. 9:10 etc.).

The wisdom of making right choices

Experience in walking with God in daily life and of growth into maturity as a believer, helps us to understand that the commandment is **good** (Rom. 7:12) and that keeping the word of God is **beneficial** for us. We come to understand that **there is wisdom in keeping the commandment**, as we see ourselves reaping the benefits of walking in holiness. So, living in holiness becomes no longer a matter of legalism, but of **living out of wisdom**. We live in holiness because we have understood that it is the right thing to do, and that we derive its benefits in our lives. So we live out of the life-applied teaching of the epistles (see Eph. 5:15,17).

We choose to walk in holiness, because we understand that sin brings us the wrong result. Keeping bad company corrupts good character (1 Cor. 15:33), and a companion of fools suffers harm (Prov. 13:20). So what do we do? We choose to associate with the wise and thereby become wise ourselves (Prov. 13:20). The simple young man of Proverbs 7:6-27 lacks judgement and chooses to surrender himself to Dame Folly's temptation. He goes *'like an ox to the slaughter'* (7:22) and afterwards suffers the consequences (7:23,26-27; 9:13-18). By contrast, other young men follow Lady Wisdom's counsel and learn wisdom from her (Prov. 9:1-6). **The things which we allow to influence our life will affect the choices we make, with beneficial or destructive consequences as a result.**

We choose to walk in holiness because we have learned to count the cost of sin before we do it. *'A man reaps what he sows'* (Gal. 6:7). **Sin does cost and it does have its reward – the wages of sin is death** (Rom. 6:23), whereas the reward of holiness is that you protect yourself from adverse consequences: *'The one who sows to please his sinful nature, from that nature will reap destruction; the one who sows to please the Spirit, from the Spirit will reap eternal life'* (Gal. 6:8). God calls us to holiness, because he is trying to protect us from the consequences of sin. Ezra said: *'I have hidden your word in my heart that I might not sin against you'* (Ps. 119:11). **These words reflect not simply the right fear of God, but also wisdom in daily living.** A man who lacks self-control is like a city whose walls are broken down (Prov. 25:28). So this man's spiritual enemy can attack his life almost at will, and gain entrance to his life (through the gaps in the protective wall, as it were) and become a squatter in his life, bringing its destructive influence into part of the man's life.

We choose to walk in holiness, because we want to be used by God. Robert Murray McCheyne said: 'A holy minister is an awful weapon in the hand of God.'[13] A believer who flirts with sin in

---

[13] http://mcheyne.info/quotes.php, accessed on 06-01-2015.

his/her life, is running the risk of being trapped in temptation by Satan. Yielding to temptation can bring oppression into our lives. We need to learn to develop the attitude towards sin that Jesus himself had. He affirmed that Satan, the prince of this world, had 'no hold' on him (John 14:30 NIV), because he 'had nothing' in him (John 14:30 AV). **Jesus did not give place to sin in his life, and so Satan had no power over him.** As Cho puts it, Jesus did not have a landing ground for Satan in his life.[14] We need to deal with sin as soon as possible when we become aware of it in our lives: we need to confess it and repent of it!

In order to use us, God first has to clean us (John 15:2-4). So we learn to keep destructive influences away from ourselves, in order that God may be able to take us and use us for good in his kingdom. For example, we choose to honour God with our bodies and not to get involved in sexual sin (1 Cor. 6:12-20, Lev. 18); we do not smoke, and we are wise in the way we approach alcohol, if we do not choose to be altogether teetotal; we are wise in the amount or kind of food we eat and do not become gluttonous; we exercise regularly to keep ourselves physically fit. These are free choices we make through wisdom, in the desire to be used by God, and, of course, these choices also have beneficial consequences for our physical health. We look after our bodies, because these are the temple of the Holy Spirit and because we are limited in what we can do for God if our physical bodies are in an unhealthy state. We make wise choices which reflect biblical values, and so maintain our wholeness, health and freedom.

---

[14] Cho, Paul Y. *Prayer: Key to Revival*, Word Publishing: Berkhamsted, UK, 1985, p.105.

Control the access points of sin

The inexorable sexualization of western society in the last sixty years or so, has led to an increasing flood of sexual innuendo, images and pornography which is often graphically portrayed and can be easily accessed on the internet and in films, newspapers and magazines, TV programmes, social media, pop music videos and other sources. In the present generation, it is virtually impossible for people to remain unaffected in their minds, hearts and desires.

If we are to walk in holiness, and if family life in our homes is to remain unaffected by all this, **it is important to control the access points of such sin into our lives and homes**, as much as we can. This also goes for other kinds of sin or influences which may affect our lives or homes in undesirable ways, such as anger, substance dependency, and so on. Again, this is not legalism, but the practice of the principles of wisdom. Andrew Bonar said that 'Holiness in what we call small matters, is the surest test of real holiness.'[15] **Wise decisions lead to continuing freedom. Sin cannot affect me if I do not give it access to me.** So I choose not to give the devil a foothold in me, by making the right choices and controlling any points of access for sin in my life. Some pointers are given below:

a. You need to know yourself and to be aware of your weaknesses. It is these areas in which you will be vulnerable in your life. You need to take appropriate steps to make sure your weak points are not exposed needlessly to temptation. Learn to avoid places, situations and people through whom you can be easily tempted and where you know you are vulnerable.

---

[15] Unknown source.

b. Be careful of the thoughts you allow yourself to think and the words you speak. Similarly, respond wisely to some of the words which other people may speak to you.

c. Be careful of the company you keep and to whom you give access into your life: *'bad company corrupts good character'* (1 Cor. 15:33).

d. Before you watch a film or on-line video, and before you allow your children to watch one, check its certification and content (videos, DVDs, BluRays and TV programmes, if possible), especially for themes of gratuitous violence, drug use, self-harm, bad language, sexual content, horror and witchcraft / occult themes. Viewing such content can give ground to your spiritual enemy in your life or home.

As the popular saying goes, we are what we eat, and this is certainly true of what we imbibe from films and programmes. What we allow to enter us through our ears and eyes stays in our memory and our subconscious. It can then affect our use of language, our sexual morality, and so on. It can also affect us in terms of bad dreams or nightmares. In particular, younger children imitate what they see or hear in films in their behaviour and language. As Christians, we should not submit to the secular standard that it's okay for children of a particular age to watch films with a certain certificate. We should base our choice on biblical standards, and thereby protect ourselves and our children from content which may be spiritually destructive.

e. Similarly, wisdom is needed is our use of social media and our choice of magazines and newspapers.

f. Keep access to the internet in a place in your home where everyone can see what is being watched (cf. Ps. 33:13-15; Prov. 15:3,11). Use parental controls. Allow your children to use the internet on their mobile phones only when they are mature and discerning enough to make wise choices for themselves.

This all raises the following questions: Does society influence us and overcome us, determining for us the way in which we should live and deciding for us what our values should be? Or, do we live as salt and light in society, and, through our corporate example of practical holiness, affect society for good? Christians should not reflect society; Christians should overcome society, much as the early believers did.

Vigilance over a lifetime

The apostle Paul, as the more experienced minister, reminded and exhorted Timothy, a younger minister, about the need to walk in holiness: *'In a large house there are articles not only of gold and silver, but also of wood and clay; some are for noble purposes and some for ignoble. If a man cleanses himself from the latter, he will be an instrument for noble purposes, made holy, useful to the Master and prepared to do any good work'* (2 Tim. 2:20-21). In essence this means that **if we want to be used by God, and to be used consistently over our whole lifetime, then we must learn this lesson of holiness.** Holiness means being separated UNTO God for his use.

It is true that God loves us as we are, but it is also true that he needs to cleanse and free our hearts, and also shape and form our inward characters, if he is to be able to use us in significant ways in the work of his kingdom. Sin can indeed be forgiven, yes, **but it is freedom from sin gained and maintained that makes us into people that can be of significant use in the kingdom. An emerging leader, who privately flirts with or entertains sin in his/her heart, is numbering the days of his/her public usefulness to God. Such a person is an easy target for Satan to trip up and overthrow.** Purity of heart is a mark of commendation in a servant of God (2 Cor. 6:6 and cf. Matt. 5:8, 1 Tim. 5:2). As McCheyne said, it is a holy minister who is an awful weapon in the hand of God.

In Ephesians 6:10-18, Paul reminds us of the spiritual warfare in which we are constantly engaged in this life as believers. We need to keep our armour on, to guard our hearts and minds, to keep our eyes open, to stay awake and to be vigilant in this warfare. Slackening our bowstrings, as it were, makes it easier for our enemy to strike us.

This is particularly important when we are in a position of leadership: *'let him that thinks he stands take heed lest he fall'* (1 Cor. 10:12). Satan loves to bring about the downfall of Christian leaders in particular. King David fell into sin when he was in the prime of life and at the height of his influence as king over the lives of many people. If Satan can get a foothold in the life of a believer when they are in a position of recognized public leadership and so when they have influence over many of God's people, then not only can he cause unbelievers to blaspheme our God and mock the faith (2 Sam. 12:14), he can also cause tremendous damage, hurt and disillusionment among God's people and a loss of trust in and cynicism towards leadership, all of which can take years to heal properly.

Leaders of God's people, in particular, need to learn to be vigilant over the long-term, indeed over their whole lifetime. A temptation which you don't fall to when you are in your 30s, you may find yourself becoming vulnerable to when you are in your 50s. Among other things, some of the pitfalls which leaders have to watch out for would include illicit sexual relationships; not dealing in their own personal lives with the anger / hurt / bitterness / unforgiveness complex; a lax frame of mind when plateaued in ministry; burn-out; lack of financial integrity; and, abuse of spiritual power and influence over others.[16] By being vigilant and resolving to walk in holiness over the long-term of his life, the apostle Paul could pen his famous words at the end of his life: *'I have fought the good fight, I have finished the race, I have kept the faith'* (2 Tim. 4:7).

Some pointers to help to break the grip of habitual sin

a. Ask yourself the honest question: Do you really and actually want to have victory over this particular sin in your life? Are you prepared to renounce it and forsake it? Until you can honestly answer 'Yes' to these questions, you will not be able to develop the attitude of repentance that you need to have in order to get victory over it. Pray that God will bring you to this point.

b. If you do honestly want victory, then develop an accountability relationship with your pastor (or with his wife, if you are female) or with someone else in your church whom they would recommend. Open up to this person about your inward struggle,

---

[16] See for example Clinton, J.R. *Leadership Perspectives*, Altadena: Barnabas Publishers, 1993, p.93.

meet with them regularly to talk things through, pray with them and receive counsel from them.

c. Confess your sin to God on a daily basis and ask for the cleansing of the blood of Jesus. Receive his forgiveness for you.

d. Practise basic spiritual disciplines in your daily life in order to regularly strengthen your spiritual life.

e. Avoid places, people and situations where you are aware that you can easily become vulnerable to temptation. Embrace walking in integrity and holiness as a lifestyle. In particular, guard your heart and your mind.

f. Do not walk in carnality and spiritual immaturity, but develop an attitude towards sin which recognizes its effects on your life. Walk in an attitude of repentance as a lifestyle, and so begin to walk in freedom and maturity in your faith.

g. In your accountability relationship, open up and uncover any areas of inward shame that you are consciously aware of. Ask God in prayer that he would show you what are the roots and causes of any such areas of shame. Similarly, confess any inner hurts and wounds that you are aware that you are still carrying from the past. Such wounds and areas of shame may be connected to the particular sin you are struggling with. Command any and all evil spirits which may have gained access to your life through such things, to depart from you, and continue to take authority over them in your life. Receive and embrace God's grace and his unconditional love for you, and walk in his healing and freedom from such wounds and areas of shame.

h. Walk in God's love towards other people.

15

LEARNING TO TRUST GOD

'Trust in the LORD with all your heart and lean not on your own understanding' (Prov. 3:5)

'I will trust and not be afraid' (Isa. 12:2)

'Anyone who trusts in him will never be put to shame' (Rom. 10:11)

Reading: Exodus 15:22 – 17:7

WHEN the Lord brought the Israelites out of Egypt, intending to lead them initially to Mount Sinai through the intervening desert, it seems that he wasted no time in beginning to try to teach them the all-important lesson about learning to trust him in the practical, daily circumstances of life. **This lesson is high on God's agenda for our lives as believers**. From his perspective, taking the Israelites together through this desert as a community had a purpose – **it gave him the perfect opportunity to try to teach them this very practical lesson**. What we learn in the desert can be just as important as what we learn when things are going well. He is God of the desert just as much as he is God of the land of milk and honey!

This period of time in the history of the Israelites, recounted in the above passage from Exodus 15:22 – 17:7, consisted basically of a series of similar experiences over a period of a few weeks in which their faith was really put to the test in practical (and difficult) daily-life circumstances. These lessons in being trained to trust in God were not taught in a cosy theoretical setting, but in very practical circumstances in daily life. **It is only through practical experience, never in theory, that we can learn and master the lesson of real trust in God. So we should expect that God will use practical circumstances in our daily life to teach us this lesson of trusting him**.

Although the provision of our needs is, of course, very important, yet this process of being trained to trust God is also very important. God knows our needs and has promised to meet them, as we seek first his kingdom: *'for your Father knows what you need before you ask him… your heavenly Father knows that you need them. But seek first his kingdom and his righteousness, and all these things will be given to you as well'* (Matt. 6:8,32-33).

Don't turn away from God

This short series of experiences became a defining period for the Israelites in their history as a community. It was afterwards remembered and referred to in Scripture as encapsulating a lesson that other generations of believers need to heed and learn from (see Ps. 95:7-11 and Heb. 3:7-11).

Even though God delivered them and provided for them time after time, yet they developed a pattern of reacting negatively to what they were going through. They questioned God, beginning to murmur, to complain and even to quarrel with Moses as to why God was allowing them to go through such things (Ex. 15:24; 16:2-3,9;

17:2,4). **Their response to going through difficult circumstances revealed their own heart attitude.**

'Remember how the LORD your God led you all the way in the desert these forty years, <u>to humble you and to test you in order to know what was in your heart</u>, whether or not you would keep his commands' (Deut. 8:2 underlining my own for emphasis)

Although negative heart attitudes and responses are, at least initially, perhaps natural and to be expected in difficult circumstances, yet, for the most part, this generation of Israelites never went on to understand that this was only one part of their learning curve, and that they could press on and break through and past this negativity to a place of learning to trust and prove God, thereby learning to overcome.

Ultimately, they gave up desiring to walk with God after they kept stumbling repeatedly at the hurdle of difficult and challenging practical circumstances.   They never really understood and got to grips with this basic lesson: that God was trying to train them into becoming people who knew how to trust him in daily life issues and so would know how to overcome, and that this was the very point of the process they were going through. They never understood that, for God, process is just as important as promise, if not more so. He met their needs, but they stumbled at the process of learning to trust him:

'He humbled you, causing you to hunger and then feeding you with manna... <u>to teach you that man does not live on bread alone but on every word that comes from the mouth of the LORD</u>. Your clothes did not wear out and your feet did not swell during these forty years. Know then in your heart that as a man disciplines his son, so the LORD your God disciplines you'

KEYS TO VICTORY

(Deut. 8:3-5 underlining my own for emphasis)

In their negative response to what they were going through, they eventually hardened their hearts towards God, and Moses even changed the name of the place they were in from Rephidim to Massah (meaning 'testing') and Meribah (meaning 'quarrelling') (Ex. 17:7) which thereafter would remind them of what they had gone through at that time:

'Today, if you hear his voice, do not harden your hearts as you did at Meribah, as you did that day at Massah in the desert, where your fathers tested and tried me, though they had seen what I did'
(Ps. 95:7-9 and see Heb. 3:7-9)

In her own lifetime, Naomi also made a similar response to her suffering and difficulties when she told people to no longer call her Naomi (meaning 'pleasant'), but Mara (meaning 'bitter') (Ruth 1:20).

As followers of Jesus, we are reminded of this tendency and are exhorted not to respond in the same kind of way or to turn away from God. This experience of the Israelites in the desert is specifically referred to as a lesson that we need to heed and learn from (see Ps. 95:7-11 and Heb. 3:7-11). We are exhorted to encourage one another daily so that we do not harden our hearts, and to trust God through our circumstances: *'See to it, brothers, that none of you has a sinful, unbelieving heart that turns away from the living God. But encourage one another daily... that none of you may be hardened by sin's deceitfulness'* (Heb. 3:12-13).

To walk with God, we <u>must</u> learn to trust him

This call to learn to trust God in our circumstances and difficulties is a principle that is repeated many times in Scripture and is illustrated to us therein through the lives and experiences of many people. This implies that this is a lesson that we also need to learn – **if other generations of believers have needed to learn this, then we also need to learn it too.** Furthermore, if this lesson is repeated many times in Scripture for our learning (Rom. 15:4), then it means that we ourselves will probably only master the lesson of deep trust in God over the span of being allowed to go through several such experiences in life. We need to be <u>trained</u> into trusting God. **It takes time to really learn this lesson and to drive it home.**

Although the two concepts of faith and trust are related, yet **trust is different to faith.** Trust means learning to keep hold of someone else's hand as <u>they</u> guide <u>you</u> along a path that you yourself are not familiar with and which you might perhaps be finding difficult. This underlines the need to develop implicit confidence that this other person knows the way and that they know what they are doing. It means being willing to hand over the reins or the steering-wheel which determines the direction of our life's journey, and agreeing not to be a back-seat driver, telling them where they should or should not be driving us. **We cannot (and will not) walk with God, if we cannot trust him with the reins of our life**: *'Let him who walks in the dark, who has no light, trust in the name of the LORD and rely on his God'* (Isa. 50:10).

So how will <u>you</u> respond?

The Israelites responded in the way they did, perhaps because their expectations of what it meant to walk with God were also wrong. **As believers, we are called to walk with God through life, through ALL of life, however this turns out to be**. This means that we cannot expect that walking with God will mean that life for us will somehow become a bed of roses; this is simply not true. The Israelites made the mistake of leaning on their own human understanding, and their wrong thinking led to wrong expectations and therefore also to wrong responses. They did not live surrendered lives, and so their expectations were wrong and, when difficulties arose, they turned away from God in their hearts.

We need to adopt the perspective of learning and of being trained to trust God in and through our circumstances, rather than falling into the trap of thinking merely of our own comfort and simply wanting to be delivered from our difficult circumstances. **It is through process that we learn the more valuable lessons involved in trusting God, and this is a major key to longer-term victory in our lives**.

Somebody once made the point that difficulties can drive us deeper into the heart of God, <u>or</u> they can drive us away from him into bitterness, if we allow them to. **So, if we are to walk with God through the whole of our lives, then how we respond to practical daily life difficulties is a vital issue**.

The stronger the wind blows, the greater the need for a tree to put down deeper roots. Daily life circumstances are a call to exercise faith in God and in the promises of his word. Instead of complaining like the Israelites, Moses prayed and sought the Lord for his deliverance (see Ex. 15:25; 16:4,11; 17:4-6). Similarly, on other occasions in their later history, the Israelites were exhorted by their kings and prophets to seek God in times of national crisis, and, as they did this in repentance and trust, God delivered them in answer to their prayers.

If we are to continue to walk with God through the whole of our lives, then God needs to be the God of the whole of our lives. If our faith is to continue to the end, then it has to interface with the <u>whole</u> of our life, or else it will fail at some point. Life can sometimes be tough, and often it is issues of daily living and relating which defeat people. **The problem is life itself, not God.** So we need to surrender ourselves to him and to agree with him that we will walk with him through ALL of life, that we will 'do life' with Jesus. Then when difficulties come, as indeed they inevitably will, we will learn to hold his hand, trust him and walk with him through them.

We need to trust God both IN and THROUGH our circumstances (Isa. 50:10). Trusting God is a choice we make, based on the fact that we have understood that he is trustworthy. He is not capricious; he has integrity and will indeed see us through. Only this kind of right thinking, 'trusting in the Lord with all our heart,' will produce the right attitude and the right response in difficulties. Then we do not stumble or get stuck at the hurdle of circumstances or unanswered questions. We overcome by walking with him through them.

Seek strengthening grace

So, as we are going through our difficulties and trusting God, we need to resolve that we will seek God for his inward strengthening grace in our hearts, which will be sufficient for us (2 Cor. 12:9). As we do this and then begin to inwardly experience his grace and peace in our hearts, we find that we overcome any negative heart attitudes and wrong responses that we have, together with any associated fear, worry and anxiety (Isa. 40:31, Phil. 4:6-7). We draw strength from his word as we read and meditate on it and from his presence as we seek him in prayer. **God's strengthening grace and promises are there so that the process we are in does not become overly discouraging.** We can also find strength as we talk and pray with other believers who have learnt this lesson and can encourage and support us through our circumstances (Heb. 3:13).

Growth through circumstances

An important principle in the Scriptures is that **God can work good out of difficult circumstances** (Rom. 8:28). If we respond positively with trust towards him and learn to depend on him, seeking his face, he can then use these very circumstances to draw us and keep us closer to himself as he sustains us with his grace and strength as we go through the difficult time.

The net result of all this, is that our ongoing relationship with God grows closer: we grow in faith and mature in our walk with God; we grow in our understanding of his word and ways; our roots grow deeper into him; we develop greater levels of trust and faith, and we often see and experience God working for us in answer to prayer. This then encourages us to trust him the next time we go through difficulties. We can also testify to other believers of how we have grown and how we have seen God working, and we can encourage them as they too face learning the same lesson in their own lives. We are learning that **God CAN indeed be trusted!**

16

THE PROMISE COMES BY FAITH

'Therefore, the promise comes by faith, so that it might be by grace and may be guaranteed...' (Rom. 4:16)

'For we walk by faith, not by sight' (2 Cor. 5:7 AV)

Reading: Romans 4:16-21

THE Bible is replete with many outstanding examples of overcoming faith. Instances that come to mind might perhaps include the Roman centurion whose servant was very sick and dying, but who was healed by Jesus (Matt. 8:5-13); the prophet Elijah who believed God for the provision of his daily needs during a time of prolonged drought in Israel (1 Kings 17), and the Shunammite woman who believed God for the resurrection of her dead son through the ministry of the prophet Elisha (2 Kings 4:8-37), and so on.

However, the person that is held up to us as a paradigm or model of what it means for us to believe and attain the promises of God is Abraham, our father in the faith (Rom. 4:16). Abraham was the example of walking in faith and righteousness that the Israelites were exhorted to look to and emulate (Isa. 51:1-2).

The record of Scripture tells us that God revealed himself to Abraham and gave him a promise, that he would have a son and thereafter become the father of many nations. In its initial form, this promise was first given to him when he was about 75 years old (Gen. 12:1-3,7). As the years passed and the promise was not fulfilled, he was then faced with the challenge of how it would be fulfilled in his life. On at least two occasions, Abraham questioned God about the fulfilment of this promise, and God repeated the promise to him (Gen. 15:1-21, 17:1-22). We also know, of course, that in the meantime he did have a son, Ishmael (through Hagar, the servant of his wife Sarah), but Ishmael was not to be the fulfilment of God's promise to him. The promised child was to be born through Sarah.

By the time Abraham had become 99 years old and his wife Sarah was herself 90 years old and still barren, it had become clear to both of them that it was a physical impossibility for them to give birth to a son of their own. Abraham was by then *'past age'* and his body *'was as good as dead.'* Similarly, Sarah was *'past the age of child-bearing'* and her womb *'was also dead'* (see Gen. 18:11, Rom. 4:19, Heb. 11:11).

However, it was after God yet again repeated his promise to them in Genesis 18:9-14 that Abraham experienced what is called 'overcoming faith' and the power of God worked in them to make it possible for Sarah to conceive and give birth to Isaac. **Faith was the bridge which took them from the impossibility of barrenness, to the fulfilment of God's promise to them**.

184

The principles enumerated in Romans 4:16-21 about how Abraham believed God for the fulfilment of his promise, are the nearest the Bible comes to an exposition of the basic principles of overcoming faith. Firstly, when confronted with the fact that, from a natural human perspective, it was impossible for God's word to be fulfilled, Abraham did not live in denial of this fact. **Faith does not live in denial of facts.** Abraham faced this fact squarely in the face, and yet, secondly, he continued to believe, basing his expectation on the clear word of God's promise to him (v18). **Overcoming faith bases itself on the word of God spoken into our lives.** Abraham continued to believe in God's ability to fulfil his promise, against all human hope (v18). **God's promises work in the face of human impossibilities.**

In fact, it is probably correct to think that God delayed the conception and birth of Isaac, specifically so that Abraham and Sarah would not think that it was they who had somehow brought about the fulfilment of the promise of God. It seems that God waited until it was humanly impossible, and <u>then</u> he acted to fulfil his word. Afterwards everyone would know that it was God who had fulfilled his word, not they.

Continuing to believe, Abraham, thirdly, did not allow his faith to waver through unbelief. The words in v20 literally mean that **he did not withdraw from or give up on the promise of God through human unbelief.** He considered that God would be faithful to his word and so he would fulfil it (Heb. 11:11). **Faith knows that God is faithful and that he keeps his word.** He did not allow what he could see, to knock his faith down. In fact, fourthly, the opposite happened. His faith in God was strengthened and he gave glory to God (v20). **Faith overcomes doubt and unbelief and presses on**

for the fulfilment of God's word. It gives a resounding answer to the question: *'Is there anything too hard for the LORD?'* (cf. Gen. 18:14).

When it says that Abraham 'gave glory to God' it means that he got to the point where he truly knew in his spirit that God could <u>and</u> <u>would</u> fulfil his promise. As he continued to fix his mind and heart on the promise of God, he overcame any doubt and unbelief still within him. He truly believed deep in his heart that God could indeed give life to the dead (v17). He also came to understand that God calls things that are not as though they were (v17). **In his spirit, Abraham perceived the spiritual reality of what God had called into being through his promise, but which was not yet manifested in the visible, physical world**, and so he was inwardly certain of what he could not yet see outwardly. This is indeed the way in which the Bible itself defines faith in Hebrews 11:1. The Amplified Bible expresses it this way:

> *'Now faith is the assurance (the confirmation, the title deed) of the things [we] hope for, being the proof of things [we] do not see and the conviction of their reality [faith perceiving as real fact what is not revealed to the senses]'* (Heb. 11:1)

In the words of 2 Corinthians 4:18, Abraham was now fixing his eyes on what was as yet still unseen, rather than on what he could physically see. This deep, inward conviction and assurance strengthened his faith and he became *'fully persuaded'* that God had the power to do what he had promised (v21). So his heart was filled with praise to God for what he was going to do. The narrative records that, about a year later, God's promise to them was indeed fulfilled, at the very time God had promised him (Gen. 18:14, 21:1-

2). **Overcoming faith guarantees the fulfilment of God's promise** (Rom. 4:16).

Overcoming faith

It should be clear from the above that when the Bible uses the word 'faith,' it is not referring to mental credence or an acceptance of truth or facts which is merely intellectual. Neither is it referring to what is commonly called 'blind faith,' i.e. the willing acceptance of something without any reasonable intellectual basis for believing it. The Greek word *pistis* means 'to have a conviction based on confidence,' and it indicates a personal relationship to the object of this confidence. It therefore involves a conscious act of the human spirit to rest in and rely on another.

In its biblical sense, **faith is our *spiritual* response to and our embracing of the *spiritual* revelation** which comes to us through the inward work of the Holy Spirit when we hear the word of God and receive it into our lives. Faith then is the spiritual link between us and God which creates a living relationship with him, much as a wire cable is the link between a kettle and the plug-socket which is its source of mains power. To change the metaphor, faith is the vehicle which brings God's salvation experientially into our life.

'Overcoming faith' is the term used to describe acting or standing in faith, or stepping out in faith, in circumstances or challenges in daily life. In this sense, therefore, we are not referring to initial faith for salvation (such as in Eph. 2:5-6 or Heb. 6:1). The key verse which encapsulates the meaning of overcoming faith is found in Hebrews 11:6, as follows:

'And without faith it is impossible to please God, because anybody who comes to him must believe that he exists and that he rewards those who earnestly seek him' (Heb. 11:6)

Several things are clear from this verse:

a. a prerequisite to exercising overcoming faith is that we must believe God exists. This is, of course, axiomatic.

b. we must also believe that God rewards those who <u>earnestly seek</u> him. The Greek word *ekzeteo* used here literally means 'to seek out' and implies a strengthened form of seeking which keeps on seeking until it finds, rather than giving up at some point. It is a seeking which knows perseverance and will not be denied.

c. overcoming faith <u>pleases</u> God. Put another way, a heart attitude of true, practical faith pleases God. He likes it when people exercise faith in him, because this gives him the opportunity to work on their behalf. Similarly, the apostle Paul speaks of having an attitude of faith: *'With that same spirit of faith we also believe and therefore speak...'* (2 Cor. 4:13).

It was overcoming faith which many people in the gospel stories exercised towards Jesus in his ministry, and on several occasions it is recorded that he commended them for it. It is the kind of faith which Jesus referred to in his question in Luke 18:8, *'However, when the Son of Man comes, **will he find faith on the earth?**'*

The power of overcoming faith

Overcoming faith links a person to God in human situations and sees his power released to act. It embraces the promises of God and sees their fulfilment. Jesus was pleased when people came to him, believing him to meet their needs, and, as stated above, he often commended them for it. He gave people according to their faith (e.g. Matt. 8:13, 9:29; Luke 5:20) and told people that it was their faith that had saved or healed them (e.g. Mark 5:34, Luke 18:42). He also encouraged their faith when they were struggling with unbelief. For example, he told the man who had a son with an evil spirit that *'Everything is possible for him who believes'* (Mark 9:23). Jesus evidently enjoyed hearing testimonies from people of how the power of God had worked in their lives (e.g. the testimony of the woman with the issue of blood, related in Mark 5:29-34). **He enjoyed seeing people walking in faith**.

Jesus emphasized the unlimited power of overcoming faith on several occasions. He told his disciples that even a small grain of faith could move a mountain, and that nothing would be impossible for them (Matt. 17:20-21, Mark 11:22-23). On occasion, they would have felt mildly rebuked by him for having only 'little faith' when they had given place to doubt in their minds (e.g. Matt. 14:31 and cf. Mark 11:23). The disappointing unbelief which he encountered on his visit to Nazareth made it impossible for him to do any mighty works there (Mark 6:5-6). **Jesus knew the power of faith and he expected and wanted believers to exercise it.**

In seeing overcoming faith working in any given situation or circumstance, **the key issue is that we perceive that it is exercising faith in God which will see us through**. Believing that God can or wants to act in the situation is a stimulus within our spirit to then exercise faith in him and believe him to work. So we respond to the situation by exercising faith in him, and our faith in him is then vindicated by seeing him act on our behalf.[17] The mindset of the woman with the issue of blood is a good example of this: *'When she heard about Jesus,... she thought, "If I just touch his clothes, I will be healed."'* So she exercised her faith, came up to him through the crowd, took hold of his garment, and was instantaneously and completely healed by the power of God (Mark 5:27-29).

God's purpose: to form people of faith

God desires to form us into people who know how to exercise overcoming faith, to trust and believe him in life's circumstances, and to see his power to act in situations. The verse in Hebrews 11:2 (NIV) tells us that our ancestors and forebears in the family of faith were commended for their faith. The NKJV version renders this verse as: *'for by [faith] they obtained a good testimony.'* It is this testimony of theirs, this example of what overcoming faith did for them in their own generation, which still speaks to us today and inspires us to believe God for ourselves. Inspiring our faith is, of course, the whole point of Hebrews chapter 11 in recounting to us the experiences of the so-called 'heroes of faith.' Paul calls Abraham *'the father of us all'* (Rom. 4:16) and it is interesting that he refers to us as being those who *'are of the faith of Abraham,'* i.e. we believe God with the same kind of overcoming faith that he had. We are cut from the same spiritual rock and hewn from the same spiritual quarry (Isa. 51:1-2), **so we are exhorted to emulate the faith of our father Abraham and of our forebears in the faith.**

---

[17] See Clinton's discussion of the faith check in Clinton, J.R. *Leadership Emergence Theory*, Altadena: Barnabas Publishers, 1989, p.143.

Experiencing overcoming faith is exciting and can sometimes be spectacular, just as it was for people in the Bible. It works in the impossible and can change the unchangeable. As we grow in faith and confidence in our walk with God, and as we begin to relate what we are learning from the Bible to our daily life experience, we will, sooner or later, be encouraged to believe that God will be the same God for us as he proved himself to be for the people whose experiences are recorded in the Bible. This helps us to begin to take small steps of faith in believing God to work in issues and situations in life. Early on in his walk with Jesus, Peter took a step of miracle-working faith when he stepped out of the boat and walked on water, although when he took his eyes off Jesus, he inevitably began to sink, of course (Matt. 14:28-31). Seeing God working in response to our faith convinces us in experience that God's promises and his faithfulness are true and that we can rely on them. It gives us strong encouragement and deep assurance in our walk with God.

Furthermore, if we know and are proving in our experience that God is faithful to his word and promises, not only are we building a strong foundation for our spiritual lives and building testimonies that we can share with other people to encourage them, it also builds our confidence to then take greater steps of faith and to believe God for greater things as we go on through life. Leaders in particular need to learn how to take steps of faith if they are to see growth in their ministry and to see God's work growing and expanding through them. **Leaders need to master this principle of overcoming faith.** David first had to learn how to deal with a bear and a lion when they attacked his sheep, before he was then ready to take on the challenge of Goliath (1 Sam. 17:34-37).[18]

---

[18] ibid, p.143.

This suggests the following points as we continue to grow in faith:

a. we will only grow in overcoming faith as we apply our faith practically to the circumstances of our life;

b. we cannot walk through life with God, and therefore we cannot co-work with him either, if we cannot trust him in our circumstances and life situations, or to provide for us;

c. we cannot take anyone further than we have gone ourselves. We cannot exhort someone to trust deeper in God than we have trusted in him ourselves. We cannot preach faith in God to others, if we do not exercise faith in God ourselves in our own life circumstances.

Strengthening our faith

Perhaps the most difficult aspect of the process involved in believing God through overcoming faith, is that of the inward battle which we often experience between faith and unbelief, between the promises of God and our own inward questions or doubts, particularly if the situation lasts for some time. This inward battle is epitomized in the heart-cry of the father of the boy who had an evil spirit: *'I do believe; help me overcome my unbelief!'* (Mark 9:24).

It is clear from the narrative in the book of Genesis and from the words of Romans 4:20 that Abraham also experienced such an inward battle. In translating the Greek word *diakrino* to express this internal struggle in Romans 4:20, the NIV says that *'he did not waver'* and the AV renders it as *'he staggered not.'* What this means is that despite his struggle, Abraham did not give place to unbelief and give up on God's promise to him; he did not decide against it or withdraw from it. Abraham won the battle over his inward struggle: it says that he was *'strengthened in his faith'* (Rom. 4:20).

In order to strengthen our faith and overcome unbelief, we need to know and rely on the faithfulness of God in our situation (cf. Ex. 34:6) and to continue to 'earnestly seek' him (Heb. 11:6). As stated above, the Greek word *ekzeteo* here means to 'seek God out' and implies a strengthened form of seeking. God truly does reward *'those who earnestly seek him'*; he is indeed *'a rewarder of them that diligently seek him'* (Heb. 11:6 NIV and AV).

Seeking God's presence in this way, and regularly practising spiritual disciplines in order to keep our faith strong and healthy, will allow the Holy Spirit to feed, sustain and inwardly strengthen our faith, as he encourages us through the word of God. **Faith comes through the word** (Rom. 10:17), so we need to constantly feed ourselves on the word of God and to stand on his promises to us in the situation, in order not to be overcome by unbelief. Abraham stood on the repeated promises of God to him. As another example, Jesus was on his way to Jairus' house to heal his dying daughter, when Jairus received the news that his daughter had died and there was therefore no point in troubling Jesus anymore. Jairus could have given up in unbelief at this point. However, Jesus **ignored what they said** and strengthened Jairus' faith by encouraging him to continue to believe with his words, *"Don't be afraid, **just believe"*** (Mark 5:36).

So, if you sense that God would have you take a step of faith in your circumstances, or that you need to believe him to give you a breakthrough in your situation, then don't be afraid to stand on his promises and believe him. He is a faithful God who can work powerfully on your behalf. He will give you the same or similar promises that he gave to Joshua: *'I will give you every place where you set your foot... I will be with you; I will never forsake you... Be strong and courageous. Do not be terrified; do not be discouraged, for the LORD your God will be with you wherever you go'* (Josh. 1:3,5,9).

17

LIVING OUT OF OVERCOMING GRACE

'Let us then approach the throne of grace with confidence, so that we
may receive mercy and find grace to help us in our time of need'
(Heb. 4:16)

'You then, my son, be strong in the grace that is in Christ Jesus'
(2 Tim. 2:1)

Reading: Matthew 5:43-48 and Luke 6:27-36

ONE of the most important – and indeed vital! – lessons that we all as believers need to learn as we continue in our walk with the Lord, is that of **learning to experience the overcoming grace of God as we need it in different situations in life**. This again is not a lesson that we should understand only in theory, and so pay mere lip service to in practice, as though we have learnt all about the overcoming grace of God once we have heard some teaching on it. No, this is a principle that works and proves its power and truth in practice as we actually learn how to experience overcoming grace when we need it.

An interesting experience that I had in regard to overcoming grace happened early in my missionary career when I was living in a particular country in Eastern Europe in the period before the Berlin Wall fell. At that time these countries were still police states and their ruling regimes were communist and atheistic. I was living with an extended family, renting a room in their large house. With all the economic problems of the time and with several mouths to feed, they needed some extra income, and my living with them provided them with this.

Although I could not yet communicate properly in the local language, yet it was not long before I discovered that there was a marked degree of lying, overcharging, manipulation and deception in the local culture, particularly when it came to money. In those early days, I was often the vulnerable, unwitting and frustrated victim of other people's rapacity. Other local ex-patriates were also having similar problems, so there were others in the same boat that I was in.

I tried my level best wherever I went not to get 'ripped off,' but these things continued over several months and reached a climax one day when yet another financial injustice was laid upon me which led to a confrontation between me and another local person. In my heart, I was upset, angry and resented these kinds of things. I was fed up with people simply and shamelessly looking upon me as a gullible source of easy money.

However, I was aware that I had arranged to go to preach the following weekend in a church (up in the north of the country) in which an old friend of mine was an elder. With all the resentment and hard feelings I was carrying within me, I knew that I was in no fit state to preach to others. So, over the next few days, I began to seek the Lord, both to help me in the state I was in and to prepare myself for preaching.

As I sought the Lord, he led me to the passages in Matthew 5:43-48 and Luke 6:27-36 and began to challenge me to love my enemies and to pray for those who mistreat me, or at least those people who I perceived were such at that moment. I came face to face with the fact that in my own natural human weakness and in the state that I was in in my heart, I could not love them, neither pray for them nor bless them. Indeed, all I was thinking and wanted was just the opposite of these things! And it was no good thinking of simply running from the situation and moving away, as the same problem would undoubtedly occur again elsewhere. No, I had to stay and sort this thing out properly within myself. If this was part of what it meant for me to be a cross-cultural missionary at that time, then I had to get victory over it.

As I continued to seek the Lord and stay in his presence over the next few days, confessing my own strongly resentful feelings and attitudes, and asking for his forgiveness, I began to experience the Lord strengthening me within and beginning to free me and wash me clean from the negative things in my heart. Within three days or so of seeking the Lord for a set time every day, I found that he had freed me from what was in my heart and had replaced it with his own grace and love, and I began to pray freely and genuinely for the person who had offended me recently, that the Lord would truly bless and reveal himself to that person. It was the Lord ministering his grace to my heart, and I was freed and cleansed within, harbouring no ill-feeling. So I decided that, because these passages in Matthew 5 and Luke 6 were so fresh in my own heart and life, I would preach from them the following Sunday.

When Sunday came, I set out early in the morning and travelled up north, arriving at my friend's home in the early afternoon. As was

197

their custom, I was ushered into the room where they often met with guests and friends. I sat down and was given a coffee to drink while I waited for my friend to come. However, when he walked into the room, I got a real shock. I had never seen him in such a state. He had a broken nose and two black eyes, and looked very discouraged indeed.

After we had greeted one another, we sat down and he told me what had happened to him. As he was travelling around in his car one day that week, he had been stopped by a couple of plain-clothed police officers who dragged him out of his car, and, without any reason at all apart from the fact that he was a well-known local Christian leader, beat him up before then driving off in their own car, leaving him lying on the road. As he spoke, I could see how shaken he was by this experience, and how hurt, frustrated and angry he was within himself. He trembled physically and wept as he told me his story, and I could see just how difficult it was for him to speak calmly about it. I spoke little, words seemed cheap...

I began to ask myself how could I possibly preach on those passages in Matthew 5 and Luke 6, when my friend would be on the first row of the church right in front of me, in just an hour or so? I knew that the believers in the church would think that I had only decided what to preach on, after I had met my friend and seen what had happened to him, and that I had chosen this particular message just for him. I was challenged within myself. Should I preach it, or not? It was certainly a relevant message to give, and yet it seemed inappropriate and too direct in view of what he had been through. Let someone else preach this message today, I thought, just don't let it be me! Although my own experience that week had been very real, and certainly I had needed the Lord's grace to minister to me, yet my friend's own experience seemed much, much harder than my own.

However, I decided to go ahead and preach what I had prepared. And it was so relevant. Everyone understood it, and many of them were looking over at my friend as I preached it. I told them what I had experienced myself that week, so that they did not think that I was preaching it just for him. He listened with tears in his eyes and knew that it was the Lord's word for him. He too needed the overcoming grace of God at that time, and in a deeper way than I had experienced it myself, but still the same grace of God working in his heart at his own point of need, to free him and heal him from the inward hurt, anger and resentment that he was feeling at that time.

God is a God of grace

God's grace, his unmerited favour towards us, is the moving cause by which he makes his salvation available to us. Without this grace, there would be no salvation. God's grace moved him to act to overcome our sin and to pour his love and mercy out on us in Christ (Eph. 2:4-5,7-8; Titus 2:11). Where our sin abounded, his grace towards us did much more abound (Rom. 5:20). He chose to freely give and indeed lavish this incomparable, glorious grace upon us, overcoming and washing our sins away completely through the redemption that Jesus provided for us (Eph. 1:3-8), so that, just as sin reigned in our lives, now grace might reign in us (Rom. 5:21).

So, when we experience this grace of God in our lives, **it changes us, and its results are evident for others to see.** When Barnabas arrived in Antioch, he *'saw the evidence of the grace of God'* (Acts 11:23). The life of the early community of believers was characterized by *'much grace'* and we are told that this grace was very practically demonstrated in meeting people's needs (Acts 4:33-35).

Furthermore, God's continuing grace towards us sustains us in our walk with him. The apostle Paul emphasized this in his short greetings at the beginning and ending of his epistles (see Rom. 1:7, 16:20; 1 Cor. 1:3, 16:23; etc.). God continues to forgive our sins and failures in daily life, as we confess them (1 John 1:9). However, in order that grace might reign in our lives, we need also to come to know his grace empowering us within, through the inward presence of the Holy Spirit, in situations in life. The Holy Spirit <u>is</u> the Spirit of grace (Heb. 10:29). So we need to **grow in grace** (2 Peter 3:18). **The grace of salvation and forgiveness has to become also the grace of overcoming in situations of life. Experiencing this overcoming grace of God is the secret of many spiritual victories in daily living.**

Grace: the authentic mark of Christian living

It is the presence and power of God's grace working within us which is the authentic mark of Christian living. This is clear from the use of the Greek word *charis* (meaning 'grace') in Luke 6:27-36 (which parallels Matt. 5:43-48), where Jesus repeats the same question about grace three times in different ways (vv.32-34). To live in such a way that we love only those who love us, and so on, is essentially to live in a way which is no different to unbelievers, and is therefore not a mark that we are walking in Christ. We do not need grace to live like that.

This passage in Luke 6:27-36 makes it clear that it is the presence of God's grace working powerfully in and through us that enables us to love our enemies, etc. Our initial natural reaction, even as believers, to those who are our enemies, or who mistreat us, curse us, hit us on the cheek, or steal our cloak (vv.27-30) will normally be one of resentment, hatred or wanting revenge, etc. We would never love our enemy in our own human strength; it is impossible. Jesus is saying that **the way in which to overcome these kinds of natural feelings and responses is to experience the grace of God actively working in and through us**, the same grace that God himself expressed towards us when we were unbelievers ourselves.

This powerful inward presence and working of his grace is the key to loving, doing good, blessing, praying, and so on, in such situations (vv.27-31,35). When the sin of other people abounds towards us, then the grace of God working powerfully within us can abound even more to overcome their sin and its effects on us, so that we can respond out of love, goodness, blessing and prayer, etc. This takes us beyond the limitations of our human nature and is the authentic mark of what it means to be a Christian. It helps us to act and respond like our heavenly Father would, and we are then shown to be his children, as we are responding as he would respond (vv.35-36).

The key verse

The key verse regarding overcoming grace is found in Hebrews 4:16 *'Let us then approach the throne of grace with confidence, so that we may receive mercy and find grace to help us in our time of need.'*

Experiencing overcoming grace in different situations is not something which works automatically. It is not at all enduring something in our own human strength and with a false smile. It is not a theoretical concept. **It involves an actual deep change of our internal spiritual condition.**

There are four steps in this verse which are the pathway to experiencing overcoming grace and the deep, internal change which it brings about.

Firstly, **we must be consciously aware that we are in a time of need**, i.e. we are in a situation in which we are being stretched beyond our human limitations and need God's grace and strength.

Secondly, **we then come to God confidently as his children and seek to get into his presence through prayer**.

Thirdly, **we confess our human weakness and failings, and perhaps our sinful responses in the situation, so that we receive God's mercy and forgiveness for these.**

Fourthly, **we stay in his presence, communing with him for as long as it takes, until the grace that we need arises within, diffused within us by the indwelling Holy Spirit of grace, to strengthen us and to overcome the subjective internal effects of the situation upon us.** As this happens within us, fear melts away and is replaced by faith; worry and anxiety are displaced by trust and deep peace; hatred, criticism and a desire to get our own back, are displaced by God's love for people; human weakness is changed to spiritual strength (Isa. 40:31), and so on. This deep subjective change in our inward spiritual condition shows us that we are experiencing God's overcoming grace within: *'It is good for our hearts to be strengthened by grace...'* (Heb. 13:9).

These steps of Hebrews 4:16 outline to us an experiential principle which we must learn to practise as believers whenever we need to. There will be occasions when we will need to go through these steps perhaps several times before the overcoming grace we need arises within.

This lesson is so vital that believers who do not learn it or who are not self-disciplined enough to practise it when they need to, **leave themselves bereft of the very source of strength that they need**, then having only their own weak and failing human strength to rely on. This, of course, is not the Lord's intention for us. He makes overcoming grace available to us, because he knows that we need it often enough. We should keep in mind D.L. Moody's words:

'A man can no more take in a supply of grace for the future than he can eat enough for the next six months, or take sufficient air into his lungs at one time to sustain life for a week. We must draw upon God's boundless store of grace from day to day, as we need it.'[19]

Some areas of application

The apostle Paul commended the believers in Corinth on how they were excelling in different areas of their lives, and he exhorted them in particular to see grace working in their lives in the area of financial giving: *'see that you also excel in this grace of giving'* (see

---

[19] Taken from http://christian-quotes.ochristian.com, accessed on 08-01-2015.

2 Cor. 8:6-7). **Grace can change natural, self-preserving tight-fistedness into free generosity.** He then enlarged on this by making an all-encompassing, comprehensive statement that, in fact, God can *'make all grace abound to you, so that in all things at all times, having all that you need, you will abound in every good work'* (2 Cor. 9:8). Put simply, **we can know and experience God's overcoming grace in any and every area of our lives.** He is the God of ALL grace (1 Peter 5:10). Paul exhorted Timothy to not only learn this principle of overcoming grace in practice, but also to so grow in it that he became <u>strong</u> in it (2 Tim. 2:1).

a. *When you are in difficult circumstances*
Reading: 2 Corinthians 12:7-10

Paul explicitly stated this lesson of overcoming grace when he related the experience of his 'thorn in the flesh.' Three times he prayed that God would take it away from him, but, **rather than simply doing that and giving him an easier life, the Lord exhorted him to learn this deeper lesson of proving the sufficiency of the overcoming grace of God in his circumstances**: *'My grace <u>is</u> sufficient for you, for my power is made perfect in weakness'* (2 Cor. 12:9 underlining my own for emphasis).

Paul accepted and embraced this exhortation, and he evidently found that it worked in his own life and ministry. Indeed, he seems to have mastered it so well that he even said he <u>boasted</u> *'all the more gladly about my weaknesses'* and that he <u>delighted</u> *'in weaknesses, in insults, in hardships, in persecutions, in difficulties'* (2 Cor. 12:9,10). He learned that, when he was weak and in need, he had a secret source at the throne of grace where he could seek a renewal of Christ's grace and power within him, making him spiritually strong

(2 Cor. 12:10). **So he proved in experience that God's grace could always be sufficient for him whatever his circumstances**: *'for when I am weak, then I am strong'* (2 Cor. 12:10).

b. *When you are hurt or wounded*

The antidote to wounds picked up in life or ministry, is not running away from people or becoming bitter, and it is certainly not resenting God. Neither is it gossiping around and pouring out your hurts to other people. That is to miss the grace of God. **It is learning to come and seek the face of God for as long as you need, and as often as you need, and pouring out your heart to him until the inward hurt is healed completely by his grace in his presence.** Jesus is and always will be the only one whose face and presence you need to seek and stay by. He can heal you completely. **There are simply too many wounded soldiers in the body of Christ whose hearts remain unhealed.**

'See to it that no one misses the grace of God and that no bitter root grows to cause trouble and defile many' (Heb. 12:15)

God's abounding grace is ALWAYS there for us, and it will never be taken away. When we are hurt, taken advantage of, ignored, or wounded by whoever or whatever, we must learn to practise the steps of Hebrews 4:16 and to do this whenever and as often as we need. Otherwise, we simply end up falling into Satan's trap of licking our wounds in bitter isolation, until we do eventually humble ourselves and come to the throne of grace.

Knowing healing grace in this way is a lesson for a whole lifetime and it enables us to keep our relationships open and ongoing, rather than closing up and distancing ourselves from people in our hurt. When we learn to deal with bitterness by getting rid of it at the throne of grace (see Eph. 4:31), we are then in a position to follow Paul's exhortation to respond to people with grace: *'Let no corrupt communication proceed out of your mouth, but that which is good to the use of edifying, that it may minister grace unto the hearers'* (Eph. 4:29 AV underlining my own for emphasis).

The apostle Peter also referred to this all-sufficient power of the grace of God to minister deeply to our inward hurts, when he highlighted its power to restore the inward soul hurt that we experience when we undergo persecution for the faith. God's grace can restore and strengthen our hearts, and make us once again firm and steadfast in our faith: *'And the God of all grace,... after you have suffered a little while, will himself restore you and make you strong, firm and steadfast'* (1 Peter 5:10). He then exhorted his readers to stand fast in the experience of this overcoming grace: *'...this is the true grace of God. Stand fast in it'* (1 Peter 5:12).

c. *In the church family*

People who come to church are all different, have different circumstances and backgrounds, and struggle with different issues. We need to learn to see people with the eyes of God's grace and love, and not to criticize or judge superficially. God loves people. Other believers are just as much 'in process' in their walk with God as we ourselves are. Similarly, when other believers fail or fall, it is not the eye of criticism they need, but the heart of God's grace within us to minister to and pray for them.

Furthermore, our attitude towards our church leaders should be one of grace. They are never perfect, but are indeed appointed by

God for a season to lead us, care for us and teach us. Maintaining a humble, learning posture and knowing grace, will cause us to pray for them, rather than criticizing or gossiping about them behind their backs when we see their weaknesses or when they fail us. We need to pray for them, that they will have all the grace, wisdom and endurance that they need to lead us (see Eph. 6:18-20 and 1 Tim. 2:1-2).

d. *Sin in society*

As Christians we need to know grace towards unbelievers in society around us, the same grace which God expressed towards us, rather than giving in to the temptation to judge people for their lifestyle or the particular sins that characterize their lives: *'Be wise in the way you act toward outsiders; make the most of every opportunity. Let your conversation be always full of grace, seasoned with salt, so that you may know how to answer everyone'* (Col. 4:6 underlining my own for emphasis). The Pharisees tended to judge people over their lives, but Jesus told them that they themselves were simply hypocrites (Matt. 23). We need to remember that, where sin in society increases, God's grace within us as believers needs to increase all the more to overcome any negative responses we may have within us towards their sin (Rom. 5:20).

A negative attitude of criticism and judging will cause us to withhold the message of God's grace and mercy and, as a consequence, we may not seek people out to tell them about Jesus. Our message can then effectively turn into one of condemnation, and so, of course, their lives do not change. God loves people deeply, he is gracious towards them and his kindness leads them to repentance (Rom. 2:4). **God's grace can overcome the shame of any sin. Our** call as Christians is to be channels to minister God's grace into people's lives, whatever their condition or sin. The only antidote to people's sin is the good news of God's grace (Acts 20:24).

18

OVERCOMING OUR SPIRITUAL ENEMY

'For our struggle is not against flesh and blood, but against... the powers of this dark world and against the spiritual forces of evil in the heavenly realms...' (Eph. 6:12)

'Therefore put on the full armour of God, so that when the day of evil comes, you may be able to stand your ground, and after you have done everything, to stand. Stand firm then...' (Eph. 6:13-14)

'They overcame him by the blood of the Lamb, by the word of their testimony and they loved not their lives unto the death' (Rev. 12:11)

The advance of the kingdom of God

AFTER Jesus was filled with the Holy Spirit at his baptism and overcame Satan in the temptations in the wilderness, Scripture says that he returned to Galilee *'in the power of the Spirit'* (Luke 3:21-22, 4:1-14). He then travelled around *'proclaiming the good news of God. "The time has come," he said. "The kingdom of God is near..."'* (Mark 1:14-15). His ministry was marked by a significant expansion of the working of the kingdom of God and its authority and power in people's lives. The apostle Peter summed up this ministry in his well-known words in Acts 10:38 *'how [Jesus] went around doing good and healing all who were under the power of the devil...'* (cf. Isa. 61:1).

In this ministry of Jesus, the kingdom of God was forcefully advancing in offensive spiritual warfare against the dominion of darkness, *'binding the strong man'* (Matt. 12:25-29, Luke 11:21-22) and releasing people from Satan's grip on their lives. Freedom from spiritual oppression was the daily bread of the children of faith (Mark 7:24-30). Jesus' compassion for people led him to commission his twelve disciples, giving them power and authority to go out and do the same kind of ministry as his own (Matt. 9:35-38; 10:1,7-8), and later he also said to the seventy-two that *'I have given you authority to trample on snakes and scorpions and to overcome all the power of the enemy'* (Luke 10:19). It is interesting that the gospel narratives give us glimpses into the fact that demon spirits recognized who Jesus was as the Son of God and were already aware of their ultimate demise at his hands (e.g. Mark 1:24, 5:7; Luke 4:41, 8:31). Satan knows his expected end and that his time is short (Rev. 12:12).

This spiritual assault of the kingdom of God upon the dominion of darkness came to a climax in the events of the cross and resurrection, where Jesus, by his death, destroyed *'him who holds the power of death – that is, the devil'* (Heb. 2:14). This event of the cross-resurrection was the decisive victory against Satan's kingdom: the issue of sin was thoroughly dealt with; Satan was totally defeated and made a public spectacle of, and death itself was conquered (Col. 2:15; Heb. 2:14, 9:26; 1 Cor. 15). The triumph of the Lord Jesus in this crucial battle gives us the assurance that Satan's dominion in this world and his rule over people's lives will indeed be finally overcome and conquered once and for all.

The exaltation and reign of Christ

A key truth which needs be grasped to help us in gaining victory over our spiritual enemy is that of the ascension, exaltation and reign of Jesus. This is more than knowing that Jesus rose from the dead and has gained the victory over death. It is being clear that, forty days after his resurrection, Jesus ascended through the heavens (Heb. 4:14) and was exalted to the highest place, the right hand of the Father, far above every principality and power and far above every name that can be named, and there began his present reign as king of kings and lord of lords, with all things placed under his feet (Eph. 1:19-22, Phil. 2:9-11, Heb. 1:3-13). It was then, after his exaltation, that king Jesus sent the Holy Spirit on the day of Pentecost, who birthed the Church into existence and began to apply to the lives of human beings the completed work of Christ's redemption.

From that time forward, the kingdom of God on earth began to advance in power offensively through the Church, under the leadership and empowerment of the Holy Spirit, who was a divine witness within believers of the exaltation of Christ (Acts 2:33,36) and who demonstrated this complete victory of Christ through these early believers. The narrative of the book of Acts tells us how the gospel moved powerfully from Jerusalem to Rome, freeing people from the dominion of darkness and bringing many into the kingdom of God's Son, Jesus. King Jesus is still presently working today in this world to advance his kingdom in the lives of people everywhere, and is awaiting the day when the victory of his kingdom will have been established and all his enemies will have been made his footstool (Ps. 110:1-2, Acts 2:34-35, Heb. 1:13).

When Jesus gave the Great Commission to the early disciples, he promised to be with them unto the end of the age as the presently reigning king of kings: all authority and power in heaven and on earth has been given to him (Matt. 28:18-20). So the Jesus we love, serve and work for is not simply the Jesus who gained our redemption at the cross, nor is it simply the Jesus who conquered death by leaving behind an empty tomb. It is indeed BOTH of these, but it is also and necessarily the reigning king Jesus of John's vision in Revelation ch. 1 whom we serve, the Jesus who holds the keys of death and Hades and who is the ruler of the kings of the earth (Rev. 1:5,12-18).

This king Jesus is the One who has commissioned and empowered us to work to spread and establish his kingdom in this world, overcoming the powers of the enemy. It is now, through the Church, that the manifold wisdom of God will be made known to the rulers and authorities in the heavenly realms (Eph. 3:10). It is in this exalted king Jesus that believers are described as being 'in Christ,' particularly in the book of Ephesians: we died with him (Rom. 6:4-5), we were raised with him, being made alive with him (Rom. 6:4-5,8; Eph. 2:5; Col. 3:1-2) and we have also been raised with him and are seated with him in heavenly places (Eph. 2:6). **This is the position from which believers should recognize that they operate in the here and now**: from a position of complete victory already won in Christ, and which now needs to be applied and gained in this world through the ministry of the Church. Our calling as believers is to work together with king Jesus, empowered by the Holy Spirit, to further advance this victory of his kingdom in this world.

Reading: Ephesians 6:10-20
Daily life on the field of battle

Hence, walking with king Jesus in daily life, and particularly if we are involved in ministry, necessarily means being engaged in spiritual warfare. As believers, we must understand and accept as axiomatic the fact that we do have a spiritual enemy who is intent on attacking, disrupting and hindering us whenever he can (Eph. 6:11-12). **No believer is excluded from this**. The kingdom of God is in direct conflict with the dominion of darkness in this world (cf. Col. 1:13), and **this is an experiential fact of daily spiritual life**.

This experience of spiritual warfare in the lives of believers and churches can be seen in various passages of the New Testament, and can be appreciated through the prophetic statement to the serpent in Genesis 3:15 about the seed of the woman: *'he will crush your head, and you will strike his heel.'*

For example, the Lord Jesus discerned when Satan was attempting to influence his thinking by speaking through Peter (Matt. 16:22-23). Paul was well aware on one occasion that Satan had hindered him in his work (1 Thess. 2:18), but he also encouraged the believers in Rome that *'The God of peace will soon crush Satan under your feet'* (Rom. 16:20). The experience of the church in Smyrna shows us that it is Satan who, behind the scenes, orchestrates the persecution of churches and believers, but the believers were exhorted to overcome by being faithful even unto death (Rev. 2:10). There were examples in Jesus' ministry of people whose physical condition of sickness had been caused by unclean spirits (e.g. Luke 13:10-16), and so on.

To illustrate this warfare in the Christian life, Paul uses the image of a soldier being assailed by the 'flaming arrows of the evil one,' demonstrating thereby the need to use the 'shield of faith' to quench such arrows (Eph. 6:16). Fiery arrows wound, burn and disable. Apart from frontal assault, the soldier in the image is also vulnerable to attack from behind where he has less covering armour. In the midst of success in the Lord's work, we may also from time to time experience spiritual attacks upon ourselves, our families, our relationships in church life, and so on.

So we need to learn to live a proactive and vigilant spiritual life, and not to be passive. Passive believers are easily overcome by the enemy. We should not be so off guard that Satan can catch us by surprise. We need to be ready to face our enemy, to be alert and discerning to recognize, deal with and ward off such spiritual attacks, in order to avoid yielding to temptations to fall into sin, for example, or of ending up as wounded soldiers, particularly through such issues as hurts, unforgiveness, bitterness and broken relationships, and so on. We should be *self-controlled and alert. Your enemy the devil prowls around like a roaring lion looking for someone to devour,'* and so we need to learn to *'resist him, standing firm in the faith'* (1 Peter 5:8-9; cf. Jas. 4:7).

The armour of God

Our experience as believers on the field of spiritual battle suggests the need for us to see ourselves very much as soldiers, and, as stated above, this is the image of the Christian life which is given to us by the apostle Paul in Ephesians 6:11-17: a Roman soldier wearing armour in preparation for battle. Paul repeats his use of this image in his three-fold description of Epaphroditus as being a brother, fellow worker <u>and</u> a fellow soldier (Phil. 2:25). This image is also suggested in Psalm 110:1-3 which is prophetic of the ascension of Christ and the extension of his kingdom: *'you will rule in the midst of your enemies. Your troops will be willing on your day of battle...'* (vv.2-3).

Furthermore, in 2 Timothy 2:3-4, Paul exhorts Timothy to *'endure hardship with us like a good soldier of Jesus Christ. No one serving as a soldier gets involved in civilian affairs – he wants to please his commanding officer.'* These verses hint at essential differences between soldiers and civilians: soldiers are trained to fight, and they are ready to pay the ultimate sacrifice for their cause, if necessary. It is perhaps this which helps us to understand the principle that living a surrendered life and not loving our lives *'so much as to shrink from death'* is a key principle in overcoming our spiritual enemy (Rev. 12:11, 2:10).

So the overall picture given to us by Paul is one of readiness for spiritual battle. We are to *'put on the full armour of God...'* (Eph. 6:11). He shows us how various parts of the soldier's body are covered by different pieces of protective armour.

a. *The helmet of salvation*

The helmet protects the head, so the inference is to our mind and our thinking. A proportion of the spiritual battle that we experience as believers goes on in our mind and thought life, and it is our mind and thinking that need to be transformed and renewed in Christ (Rom. 12:2, 1 Cor. 2:16, 1 Peter 1:13). The way we think determines our attitudes, behaviour, responses and actions, and hence also the way we live, so Paul talks of demolishing *'arguments and every pretension that sets itself up against the knowledge of God,'* and taking captive *'every thought to make it obedient to Christ'* (2 Cor. 10:5).

In particular, knowing our identity (who we are in Christ) is crucially important to overcoming our enemy. We need to understand and master what God has done for us in the saving work of Christ and what he has made us in him. The truths of our identity listed at the end of chapter 2 should be known and learnt thoroughly. God sees us as we are in Christ, and, when we know and take our stand on the truths of our identity, we can disempower any doubts or accusations which Satan tries to use against us in our minds. The accuser of the brethren has been cast down (Rev. 12:10) and our lives are hidden with Christ in God (Col. 3:3).

b. *The breastplate of righteousness*

The breastplate protects the heart, the seat of human affections. Above all things, we need to be aware to guard, keep, look after, protect and preserve our heart *'with all diligence; for out of it are the issues of life'* (Prov. 4:23). Many of the decisions we make in life are determined by the desires of our heart, so our heart needs to be surrendered, clean and pure. Demas deserted Paul *'because he loved this world'* (2 Tim. 4:10). We need to learn to love righteousness and to hate and therefore avoid unrighteousness (cf. Heb. 1:9), and to love God above all other things in life (Deut. 6:5, 1 Peter 3:15). Furthermore, hurts in life can affect our hearts, and too often they cause believers to become side-lined from the field of battle. So to continue unhindered in our walk with God and in our work in his kingdom, our heart needs to be kept clean from sin, healed from hurts, and free of desires which would side-track us away from a close walk with him.

c. *The belt of truth*

The belt is fastened on around the waist area and helps to hold the armour, underclothes and weapons in place and so is essential to the soldier's preparation. Truth is not a relativistic concept, but is absolute. Jesus is the only true and complete revelation of who God is (John 14:6, Heb. 1:3). The word of God is truth (John 17:17) and so needs to be known, submitted to and held to. It is the truth which sets people free (John 8:32). By contrast, Satan is the father of lies (John 8:44). In our relationships, we are to be people of truth, speaking the truth to one another in love, so bringing about growth to maturity in the faith (Eph. 4:15).

d. *Feet shod with the readiness that comes from the gospel of peace*

The motif here is undoubtedly taken from Isaiah 52:7, *'How beautiful on the mountains are the feet of those who bring good news, who proclaim peace, who bring good tidings, who proclaim salvation...'* Paul refers to this verse again in Romans 10:14-15 where, with simple logic, he argues that people will not hear the gospel unless someone tells them about it, and those who do tell the good news need to go or to be sent in order to do this. The gospel of peace and salvation needs to be proclaimed and communicated to those who do not yet know Jesus. The soldier needs to be ready at all times to obey the call from his commanding officer to get up and go. We need to master the basic facts of the good news, and to always keep our spiritual lives fresh, so that we will be able and ready to tell others about Jesus whenever opportunities present themselves (1 Peter 3:15).

e. *The shield of faith*

The *thureos* referred to here was the large door-shaped shield used by front-line soldiers to protect themselves against arrows and spears, rather than the small shield often used in hand-to-hand sword fighting. So the image is of a front-line soldier who would often have to bear the brunt of the enemy's attacks. This shield was used for protection against objects thrown at the soldier, hence fiery arrows or spears. The shield represents our faith which needs to be alert, strong, active and expressed. We are kept, shielded, watched over and protected by God's power **through our faith** (1 Peter 1:5). This would suggest the need for us to be feeding our faith regularly so that it remains strong and active. Lack of readiness in using the shield would leave our bodies, minds and hearts more exposed to any fiery arrows that do happen to come our way from time to time.

The spiritual weapons of our warfare

In addition to describing the protective spiritual armour that we need to learn to wear, Paul also refers to the spiritual weapons that we need to learn to use in order to engage effectively in our offensive warfare against the dominion of darkness. He says in 2 Corinthians 10:2-4 that *'we do not wage war as the world does. The weapons we fight with are not the weapons of the world. On the contrary they have divine power to demolish strongholds'* (and see 2 Cor. 6:7). King David also made a similar reference when he wrote: *'Praise be to the LORD my Rock, who trains my hands for war, my fingers for battle'* (Ps. 144:1).

So, if we are engaged in spiritual warfare in the work of God's kingdom, then it is self-evident that we need to know what our weapons are and to learn how to use them. Paul's exhortation is that we should learn both how to stand and to withstand in spiritual warfare against the devil's schemes when the day of evil does come, so that we are still standing at the end of the fight (Eph. 6:11,13-14), in order that we too, like him, might finish the race with our faith still intact and strong (2 Tim. 4:7).

a. *The sword of the Spirit: the word of God*

The single offensive weapon that is mentioned in the list of pieces of armour in Ephesians 6:14-17, is the sword of the Spirit, representing the word of God (6:17). The Greek word used is *rhema*, meaning the spoken word of God. This phrase could be rendered as 'the sword which the Spirit uses is the word of God.' An example of using the written word of God as a sword is found in the desert temptations of Jesus where, when he was tempted three times by Satan, he responded in each case by verbally quoting truth from the book of Deuteronomy (see Luke 4:3-12). Doing this enabled him to overcome Satan.

The word of God is inspired by the Holy Spirit (2 Tim. 3:16) **and so it has intrinsic spiritual authority, and Satan recognizes this**. It is therefore important for us to know deeply the word of God, its truths, principles, promises and commandments, and to grow by feeding on it as often as possible. We need to remind ourselves of what it says, to be able to quote it, to stand on it and to speak it out, both in our personal lives, in prayer and when engaging in ministry.

It is a key issue in our spiritual growth to be able to discern when God is speaking to us from his word in specific situations. Such Spirit-empowered *rhema* words inspire the inward grace, faith and strength we need to stand strong in our faith and to overcome any doubts, attacks or temptations which the forces of darkness might try to use against us.

b. *Praying in the Spirit*

In Ephesians 6:18-20, Paul underlines the crucial role of 'praying in the Spirit' by emphasizing prayer five times and by his repeated use of the words 'all' or 'always' (and see also Col. 4:2-4). Men and women who have been significantly used of God in ministry have invariably been people of prayer.

To pray 'in the Spirit' presupposes that we know what it is to be filled and empowered by the Spirit. **Prayer in the Spirit is a major key to victory**. Jude also encourages us to *'pray in the Holy Spirit'* (Jude 20). The Holy Spirit can empower our prayers through praying in tongues (1 Cor. 14:14) and through the inward groanings of intercession (Rom. 8:26-27). As a form of prayer, praise played an important role in the victory of the Israelites under Jehoshaphat (see 2 Chron. 20:21-22), and, in many of his psalms, David exhorts us to praise the Lord at all times. **Spirit-empowered praise can bring breakthrough**. Prayer combined with fasting can bring victories where sometimes prayer alone does not bring about breakthrough (see Judges 20:18,23,26; 2 Chron. 20:3-4ff; Mark 9:29).

OVERCOMING OUR SPIRITUAL ENEMY

c. *Ministry in the power of the Spirit*

We are exhorted by Paul to specifically seek and pray that the charismatic gifts of the Holy Spirit might be manifested among and through us (1 Cor. 12:1,11,31; 14:1). **These gifts in all their variety are crucially important to our task.** In fact, they are the tools for the job; without them, much less can be accomplished than with them. In the ministry of the early church, we can see several of these gifts operating, e.g. miracles and healing (Acts 3:1-10, 5:15); discernment [and expulsion] of spirits (Acts 16:16-18); prophecy (Acts 11:28-30); faith (Acts 14:8-10); tongues (Acts 2:4), and so on.

It has always been God's intention and purpose that the ministry of the Church be accomplished in the presence and power of the Holy Spirit (2 Cor. 3:6,8,17). So it is natural to expect that the preaching and ministry of the word of God should be accompanied by demonstrations of the power of God (Rom. 15:19, 1 Cor. 2:4, 2 Cor. 6:7). **We are called to minister the whole gospel to the whole person in the power of the Spirit.**

d. *The name of Jesus*

The name of Jesus is the name above every other name, to which everyone in heaven, on the earth and under the earth will bow (Phil. 2:9-11). **All authority in heaven and earth has been given to him** (Matt. 28:18). Our spiritual enemy recognizes and fears the name of king Jesus (Acts 19:15). Evil spirits were subject to Jesus and to his empowered disciples (Matt. 10:1,7-8; Mark 1:24, 5:7; Luke 4:41, 8:31, 10:19), and the apostles and early believers healed and cast spirits out in the name of Jesus (Acts 3:6, 4:10, 16:18; Jas. 5:14). We are sent forth as Christ's ambassadors to minister the whole gospel to people **with the specific intention that, in his**

221

name, we might overcome the power of the enemy (Matt. 28:18-20, 2 Cor. 5:20).

e. *The blood of Jesus*

The apostle John stated that believers overcame their spiritual enemy 'by the blood of the Lamb' (Rev. 12:11). Satan both fears and hates the blood of Jesus, as it reminds him of his greatest and ultimate defeat at the cross. He was destroyed by the death of Jesus (Heb. 2:14). The blood of Jesus both seals our redemption and frees and cleanses us from all sin (Eph. 1:7, 1 John 1:7, Rev. 1:5). It deals effectively with the inward parts of our life: it cleanses our heart and frees our conscience from guilt (Heb. 9:14, 10:22). So the blood of Jesus disempowers Satan by cleaning and freeing us from issues in these inward areas which he might otherwise use to accuse or torment us. **Satan cannot overcome what the blood of Jesus has done and still does for us.** We do not belong to him and no accusation that he throws at us can stand before God. We have the deep, inward assurance that we are justified by Christ's blood (Rom. 5:9).

f. *The command of authority*

Having overcome the devil in the wilderness temptations, **Jesus exercised authority in his ministry over the works of the enemy,** and this spiritual authority was recognized by many people (e.g. Mark 1:25-27, cf. Luke 11:20). Jesus imparted spiritual authority to his disciples so that they too could overcome (Matt. 10:1), and we can see it also in Paul's ministry (e.g. Acts 13:8-11). As the commissioned servants and representatives of our exalted king Jesus, empowered by his Spirit, this authority has also been invested in us 'in Christ,' and, with discernment and wisdom, **we need to learn to exercise it in overcoming our spiritual enemy**.